UNUSUAL GUITAR SCALES FROM AROUND THE WORLD

EXOTIC GUITAR RIFFS AND LICKS

RAIF ORHEIM

RAIF ♪ ORHEIM
MUSIC PUBLICATIONS
KINGSTON, WASHINGTON

UNUSUAL GUITAR SCALES FROM AROUND THE WORLD
Exotic Guitar Riffs and Licks
by Raif Orheim

Published by: Raif Orheim Music Publications
                33727 Hood Canal Drive N.E.
                Kingston, WA 98346
Telephone: 360-638-0482
Website: www.RaifOrheim.com
E-mail: RaifOrheim@msn.com
                Follow me on Twitter @RaifOrheim
                Find Raif Orheim on Facebook

ISBN Hardbound: 978-0-9899129-0-7
Library of Congress Control Number: 2013916902

First Edition. Printed in the United States of America
10 9 8 7 6 5 4 3 2 1

Cover and Page Design by One-On-One Book Production, West Hills, California

To my daughter, Adrianna
my brother, Matthew Orheim
my mother, Michelle Carlson

ACKNOWLEDGMENTS

I would like to thank Alan Gadney and Carolyn Porter of One on One Book Production & Marketing. Also thanks to Frank Gambale for recommending Neck Diagrams software. I would like to thank Tom Leykis for your inspiration and continued inspiration. Thanks (Dad).

ABOUT THE AUTHOR

A guitar player for 25 years, Raif Orheim gives live performances, recording sessions and teaches guitar. Raif has recently been inspired to write guitar instruction books.

He became interested in unusual guitar music, when his first guitar teacher introduced him to unusual guitar scales.

He lives in the Pacific Northwest. Besides playing guitar, Raif, enjoys kayaking, cycling and spending time with his two-year-old daughter.

INTRODUCTION

This book is aimed for the intermediate beginner to the advanced guitar player. We will be exploring exotic scales from around the world, and some scales, chords, and lead guitar licks that go with each scale.

I recommend to all my students a good book on chords, such as: *Chord Chemistry* by Ted Greene, and a good Scale reference book, such as: *SCALES* by Joe Charupakorn. A wonderful music theory book aimed specifically for guitarists is *Music Theory: Everything You Ever Wanted to Know but Were Afraid to Ask* by Tom Kolb.

A very useful website full of scales, chords, chord progressions, tunings, and more is: http://www.all-guitar-chords.com.

An excellent teacher on Youtube is Andrew Wasson at http://www.andrewwasson.com. There is another guy who goes by "Rockongoodpeople." He has some great stuff for beginners as well as for more advanced players.

I hope this helps. Enjoy!

Raif Orheim

TABLE OF CONTENTS

HOW TO USE THE BOOK & GUITAR SCALES OVERVIEW

If you happened to obtain this book before having any knowledge of scales, then excellent for you! You'll be well-resourced to make the most out of all you discover from the start. Before we get into unusual scales, I will explain the basic building blocks of chords using the major scale. I will also show you the formula for the major scales so that you can see how they relate or differ from the unusual scales later on in this book.

MAJOR SCALE

The *major scale* is undoubtedly the most significant scale for you to learn. In truth, we base our complete Western harmonic arrangement off its intervallic construction. An interval is the space between two notes.

INTERVALS

An *interval* is the name we use to illustrate the space between two notes. In terms of scales, intervals are typically calculated in *half steps (*one fret on the same string of the guitar) and *whole steps* (two frets on the same string). A major scale has seven different notes (the "eighth note" would plainly be the first again in another octave), and each note is assigned a number: 1, 2, 3, etc. The *intervallic formula* for any major scale is always the same:

Whole step–Whole step– Half step–Whole step–Whole step–Whole step– Half step

So, from the first note (1) to the second note (2), the distance is one whole step, or two frets. The distance from 2 to 3 is also a whole step, or two frets. The distance from 3 to 4 is a half step, or one fret, and so on. This is demonstrated with the G major scale below:

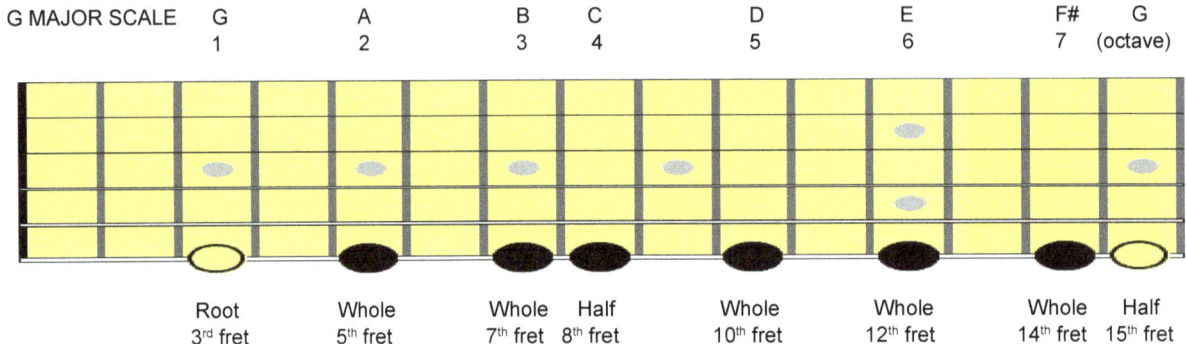

G MAJOR SCALE	G	A	B	C	D	E	F#	G
	1	2	3	4	5	6	7	(octave)

	Root	Whole	Whole	Half	Whole	Whole	Whole	Half
	3rd fret	5th fret	7th fret	8th fret	10th fret	12th fret	14th fret	15th fret

FRETS ARE THE METAL BARS PLACED ON THE FINGERBOARD.

The Tonic

The 1st degree (1) of a scale is called the *tonic;* think of it as home base. This note feels resolved when you play it. You'll hear this expression sometimes used interchangeably with "root."

You'll also notice that sometimes the tonic appears at the top of a scale in a new octave, where it can be labeled as "8," and sometimes it does not. Don't be puzzled by this. A major scale has seven *different* notes. The "eighth" note, when it does appear, is just the same as the first; this connection is referred to as an *octave.* It's sometimes useful to see this, so you can see the interval from the 7th to the tonic.

ROOT OR TONIC

The root (or tonic) is the note that names a chord, scale or arpeggio. You must memorize the location of the root. Without this location you will be lost.

SLIDE RULE THEORY

You can move any scale, chord, lick, or arpeggio up or down the neck and only the letter name will change. The color remains the same. The fingering remains the same. The root is now on another fret.

UNUSUAL OR EXOTIC SCALES

The name exotic scale is a very relative term. Usually, when people refer to a scale as being exotic they mean it is not frequently used. This may or may not be the case since somewhere in the world it might be very popular. The unusual scales in this book can be thought of as scales that are not associated to the typical major or minor scales. The majority of them have seven notes; however, a few have more or less. They offer an outstanding resource for technical creativeness/composition and work in several styles, such as pop, rock, funk, jazz, and R&B.

This book explores exotic scales and will show you the formulas for these scales so that you can see how they differ from the major scales. Before we get into the unique unusual scales, you will learn the note names on the guitar and some basic information on chords. If you already have knowledge of the notes on the guitar and basic chord formation, skip ahead.

NOTE NAMES ON THE GUITAR

6TH STRING

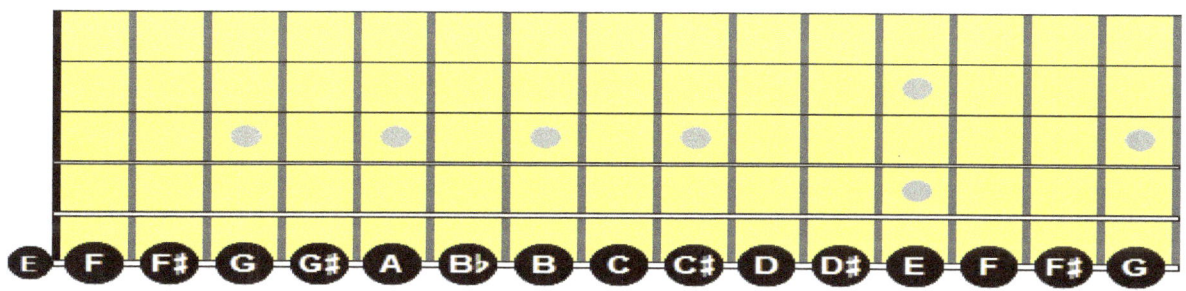

5TH STRING

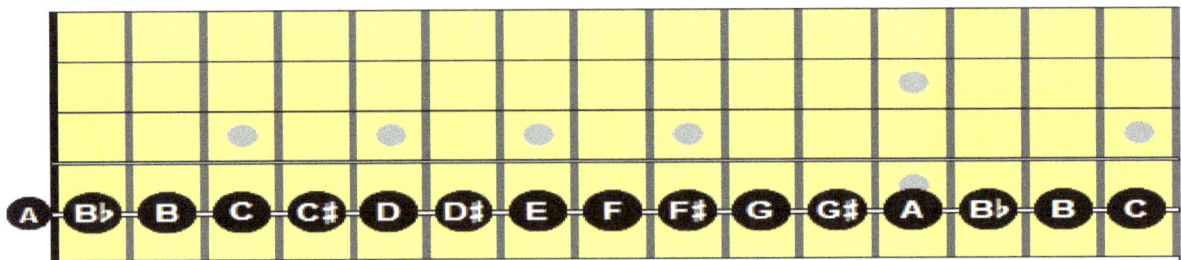

4TH STRING

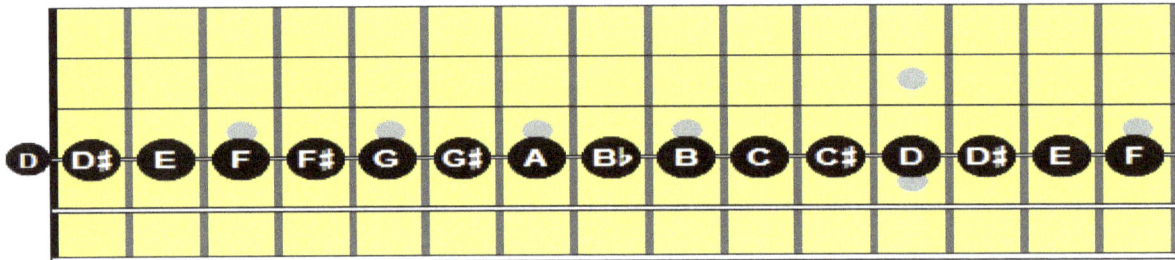

3RD STRING

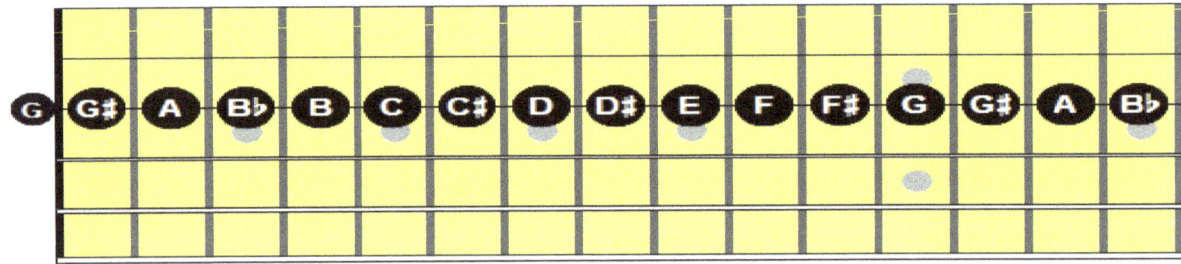

2ND STRING

1ST STRING

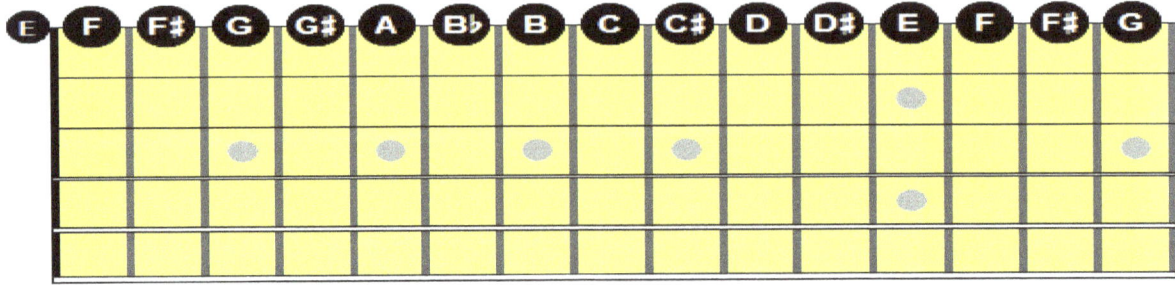

CHORD BUILDING BASICS

Chords—The Foundation of Western Music

As we've seen, music is built on a grand total of 12 possible notes, repeated in octave sets of different pitch ranges, which explains how 12 notes on a piano become 88 note choices. There are 88 different pitches, but still only 12 named notes. The same is true with guitars, Most guitars offer from about 40 to 50 different pitches, three or four octaves' worth, but still only 12 notes.

Unless you›re a really hot flatpicker or a lead guitar player, most of what you'll do on the guitar will NOT involve playing single notes in a row. Instead, you'll play chords.

The most basic complete chords—chords which complete a musical thought—are built from **three notes only**, sometimes called "**triads**," and all are found to be referring to the major scale. There are only 4 basic triads. They are built using the scale degrees shown below.

Chord Name	Scale Notes	Translation
major:	1 - 3 - 5	1st Note, plus 3rd Note, plus 5th Note
minor:	1 - b3 - 5	1st, plus flatted 3rd, plus 5th
augmented:	1 - 3 - #5	1st, plus 3rd, plus sharp 5th
diminished:	1 - b3 - b5	1st, plus flatted 3rd, plus flatted 5th (often also includes a double-flatted 7th —then called a dim7 chord)

The Major Chord—The Most Basic Chord. Most guitar players start out by learning a few major chords—usually C, F, G, A and E. But we have no idea how those chords came to be.

A major chord sounds relaxed, at rest and positive. Play any major chord and you'll see what I mean. But why is that true?

Using the formula for a major chord (1 - 3 - 5), applied to the C scale, is how we find the triad:

Major Scale	**C**	D	**E**	F	**G**	A	B
Scale Degree	**1**	2	**3**	4	**5**	6	7

So a major C chord is built on the C, E and G notes. No more, no less.

Wait a Minute, the Chords I Play Have More Than 3 Notes. Not true. It just looks that way.

But let's look at a standard C Major chord diagram.

It shows the chord notes of C - E - G, but all six strings are played. Look below the chart at the numbers, which refer to the scale degree. Remember, C is the 1 note, E is the 3 note, and G is the 5 note. So this version of a C Major chord has two 1 notes, one 5 note and three 3 notes. While only 3 are needed, this gives us the characteristically rich sound of a "big" chord.

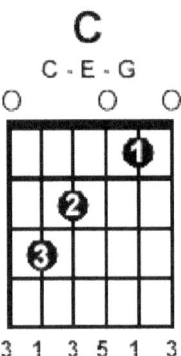

Look at the other major chord diagrams to see how all of the major chords follow this scheme—without exception.

Here are the CAGED progressions in chord-chart form. These are the first positions, most simple fingerings of the 12 chords which are used. Remember— there are other ways to finger every chord, in different places on the neck.

If you learn these 5 progressions well, and can see their relationships to each other, then you've made huge strides toward becoming a real guitar player.

● Just below the chord's name are the notes (usually just 3) which make up the chord. They are the 1 - 3 - 5 scale notes, in that order. At the bottom, each played string is identified by which scale note it represents. If it's a flatted note, it will say something like "3b."

● Xs and Os above the strings either mean don't play (X) or play open (O).

● The numbered black dots suggest the finger you should use to play that string at that fret. For some chords, like A, you may find another way which suits you, but I've tried to offer the fingerings which work well and offer flexibility in making chord changes.

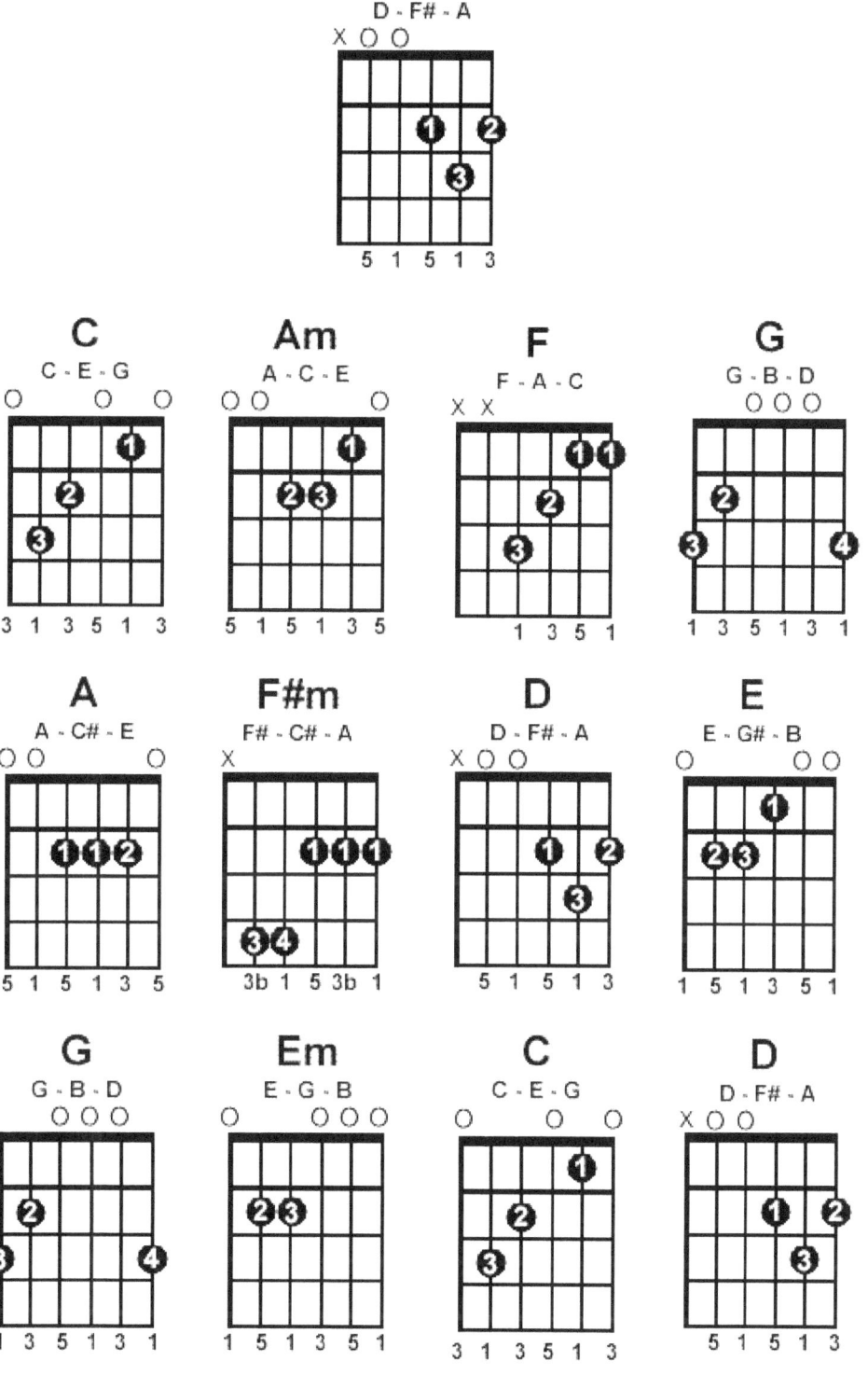

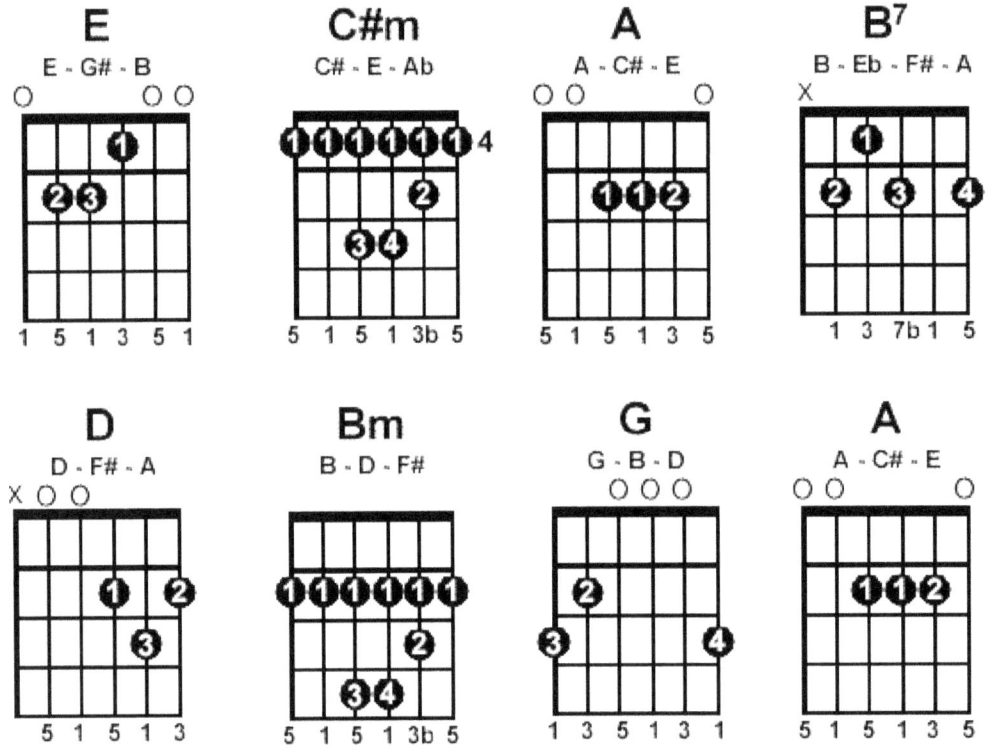

The Minor Chord

Most guitar players also begin with a few minor chords—usually **Am** and **Em**.

A minor chord sounds sad. Play one to contrast with major chords.

Using the formula for a minor chord (1 - b3 - 5) applied to the C scale, is how we find the triad:

Major Scale	**C**	D	**Eb**	F	**G**	A	B
Scale Degree	**1**	2	**b3**	4	**5**	6	7

So a minor C chord is built on the C, Eb and G notes, as shown in this diagram. Note that this is a "barre" chord at the 3rd fret (A barre chord is the technique of placing the left hand index finger over two to six strings in the fingering of a chord). Nonetheless, the formula is shown in the chart below.

You might also notice that the shape of this chord is the same as an A minor chord played in the open position. The "barre," using the index finger to span all strings at the 3rd fret simply replaces the nut.

A simple way to remember how to make any minor is to simply flat the 3rd from a major triad. So flatting the third note, E, instantly changes the chord to a minor.

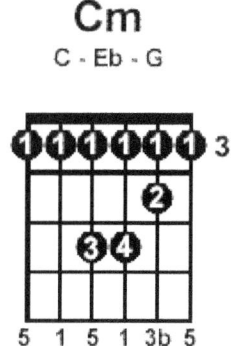

See other minor chord diagrams above.

Augmented and Diminished Chords

Most guitar players ignore these forms for the most part, so we will too—at least as they relate to the basics of chord building. But you do have the formula above if you'd like to experiment.

Adding the Seventh—The Last "Basic" Step in Building Chords.

There's one more chord you do need to understand to play most music. Its technical name is the "**dominant seventh,**" although its common name is simply "**seventh chord.**" Ignore the term "dominant" except to know that some folks may mention it occasionally.

Using the formula for a seventh chord (1 - 3 - 5 - b7), applied to the C scale, here is how we find it:

Major Scale	**C**	D	**E**	F	**G**	A	Bb
Scale Degree	**1**	2	**b3**	4	**5**	6	7

So how do you make a seventh chord? Easy—just take any major chord, identify the 7th note of the scale for that major chord, and add the **flat** of that 7th. See the C7 chord below.

A seventh chord is a major plus a flatted 7th note. It's a 4 note chord, as opposed to the triads we've otherwise talked about.

A seventh chord sounds a bit off balance, making you want to go somewhere else—ordinarily back to the root chord of the progression you're in. Sometimes called a "leading" chord, since it leads you elsewhere.

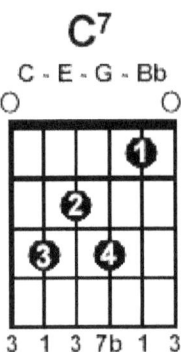

Simple, Right? There you have it—chord basics in a nutshell. These concepts are but the tip of the iceberg. However, as with an iceberg, unless you run into the whole thing, the tip may be all you ever see. This will take you a long way.

On the next page I have a list of chords and the intervals that make up those chords. You will be familiar with many of them. Such chords as Sus4, I did not cover. A Sus4 or Suspended 4 chord is the Root, perfect 4th and perfect 5th. A Sus2 or Suspended 2 chord is made up of the Root, major 2nd and perfect 5th.

CHORD SPELLING

C maj7=CEGB

C mi7=CE*b*GB*b*

Cmi=CE*b*G

C7=CEGB*b*

Cmi7*b*5=CE*b*G*b*B*b*

Csus=CFG

Cdim7=CE*b*G*b*B*bb*

Caug=CEG#

D maj7=DF#AC#

Dmi7=DFAC

Dmi=DFA

D7=DF#AC

Dmi7*b*5=DFA*b*C

Dsus=DGA

Ddim7=DFA*b*C*b*

Daug=DF#A#

G maj7=GBDF#

Gmi7=GB*b*DF

Gmi=GB*b*D

G7=GBDF

Gmi7*b*5=GB*b*D*b*F

Gsus=GCD

Gdim=GB*b*D*b*F*b*

Gaug=GBD#

A maj7=AC#EG#

Ami7=ACEG

Ami=ACE

A7=AC#EG

Ami7*b*5=ACE*b*G

Asus=ADE

Adim7=ACE*b*G*b*

Aaug=AC#E#

F# maj7=F#A#C#E#

F#mi7=F#AC#E

F#mi=F#AC

#7=F#A#C#E

F#mi7*b*5=F#ACE

F#sus=F#BC#

F#dim7=F#ACE*b*

F#aug=F#A#C##

C# maj7=C#E#G#B#

C#mi7=C#EG#B

C#mi=C#EG#

C#7=C#E#G#B

C#mi7*b*5=C#EGB

C#sus=C#F#G#

C#dim7=C#EGB*b*

C#aug=C#E#G##

B*b*maj7=B*b*DFA

B*b*mi7=B*b*D*b*FA*b*

B*b*mi=B*b*D*b*F

B*b*7=B*b*DFA*b*

B*b*mi7*b*5=B*b*DF*b*A*b*

B*b*sus=B*b*E*b*F

B*b*dim7=B*b*D*b*F*b*A*bb*

B*b*aug=B*b*DF#

E*b* maj7=E*b*GB*b*D

E*b*mi7=E*b*G*b*B*b*D*b*

E*b*mi=E*b*G*b*B*b*

E*b*7=E*b*GB*b*D*b*

E*b*mi7*b*5=E*b*G*b*B*bb*D*b*

E*b*sus=EBA*b*B*b*

E*b*dim7=E*b*G*b*B*bb*D*bb*

E*b*aug=E*b*GB

E maj7=EG#BD#

Emi7=EGBD

Emi=EGB

E7=EG#BD

Emi7*b*5=EGB*b*D

Esus=EAB

Edim7=EGB*b*D*b*

Eaug=EG#B#

F maj7=FACE

Fmi7=FA*b*CE*b*

Fmi=FA*b*C

F7=FA*b*C

Fmi7*b*5=FA*b*CE*b*

Fsus=FB*b*C

Fdim7=FA*b*C*b*E*bb*

Faug=FAC#

B maj7=BD#F#A#

Bmi7=BDF#A

Bmi=BDF#

B7=BD#F#A

Bmi7b5=BDFA

Bsus=BEF#

Bdim7=BDFAb

Baug=BD#F##

A*b* maj7=A*b*CE*b*G

A*b*mi7=A*b*C*b*E*b*G*b*

A*b*mi=A*b*C*b*E*b*

A*b*7=A*b*CE*b*G*b*

A*b*mi7*b*5=A*b*C*b*E*bb*G*b*

A*b*sus=A*b*D*b*E*b*

A*b*dim7=A*b*C*b*E*bb*G*bb*

A*b*aug=A*b*CE

D*b* maj7=D*b*FA*b*C

D*b*mi7=D*b*F*b*A*b*C*b*

D*b*mi=D*b*F*b*A*b*

D*b*7=D*b*FA*b*C*b*

D*b*mi7*b*5=D*b*F*b*A*bb*C*b*

D*b*sus=D*b*G*b*A*b*

D*b*dim7=D*b*F*b*A*bb*C*bb*

D*b*aug=D*b*FA

G*b* maj7=G*b*B*b*D*b*F

Gbmi7=GbBbbDbFb

Gbmi=GbBbbDb

Gb7=GbBbDbFb

Gbmi7b5=GbBbbDbbFb

Gbsus=GbCbDb

Dbdim7=GbBbbDbbFbb

Gbaug=GbBbD

ALGERIAN SCALE

Intervals

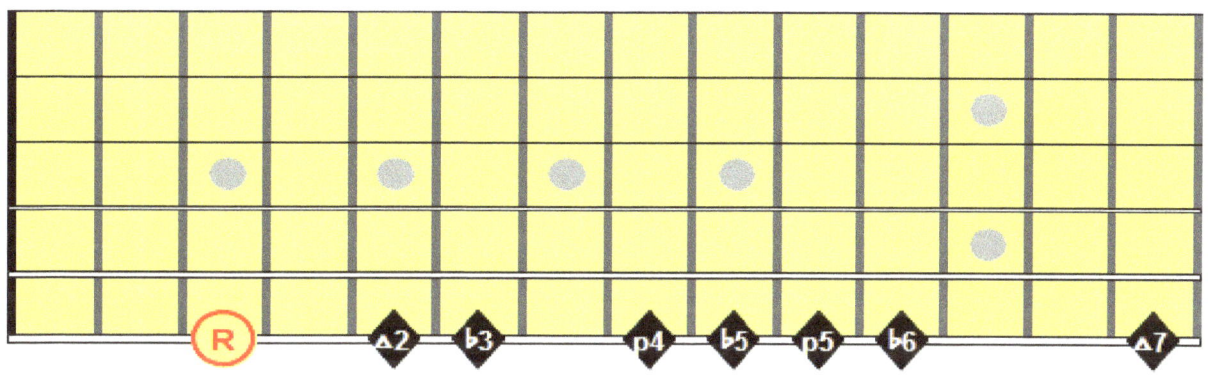

Formula: R, 2nd, b3, 4th, b5th, 5th, b6th, 7th

IN STEPS: W H W H H H W + H

STRINGED ALGERIAN INSTRUMENTS

There are six stringed instruments that are traditional in Algerian music.

The LUTH, which is a pear shaped deep body instrument similar to a mandolin

The **MANDOLIN** which is also pear shaped but more shallow bodied, are both common in the Telemencen area.

The **ERRABAB** is a long narrow stringed instrument played with a bow, similar to a violin and is also from Telemencen.

The **MANDOLE** is a shallow bodied instrument with a narrower pear shaped body, and a second type of mandolin, which has the appearance of a stylized guitar are found in other regions of Algeria.

The **EL-QANUN** is a multi-stringed instrument with a solid body and the appearance of a small harp.

The OUD is one of the most admired instruments in Arabic music. Its name derives from the Arabic for 'a thin strip of wood', and this refers to the strips of wood used to make its rounded body.

The neck of the oud, which is short in comparison to the body, has no frets and this contributes to its distinctive sound. It also allows playing notes in any intonation, which makes it ideal for performing the Arabic maqam. The most common string combination is five pairs of strings tuned in unison and a single bass string, although up to thirteen strings may be found. Strings are generally made of nylon or gut, and are plucked with a plectrum known as a risha (Arabic for *feather*). Modern strings are made of steel wound over nylon. The instrument has a warm timbre, low tessatura, and is often intricately decorated. The oud used in the Arab world is slightly different to that found in Turkey, Armenia and Greece. Different tunings are used and the Turkish-style oud has a brighter tone than its Arab counterpart. The European lute is a descendant of the oud, from which it takes its name (al-oud).

SOME HISTORY OF ALGERIAN MUSIC

Algerian music is extremely diverse; here are some of the styles of music in Africa's secondlargest country.

Andalus—a formal and much cherished style, Andalus arrived in North Africa with the removal of the Moors during the Spanish Reconquista. Often championed by the establishment as a sign of Algerian national character, it is primarily the preserve of the privileged and sophisticated, and continues to be performed in Algeria, Spain, and Morocco.

Chaabi—derived from Andalus and originating in Algiers, Chaabi contains very graceful lyrics. Very much the music of the people, Chaabi continues to call to mind memories of the motherland for the Algerian Diaspora and is performed everywhere from Parisian artistic centres to local London cafes, and looks set to be popularized by the widely-anticipated documentary film *El Gusto*, which details the reunification of an orchestra of Muslim and Jewish musicians in Algiers.

The Algerian scale is an eight tone scale. The Algerian Scale is a scale which is frequently found in a lot of Algerian, Arab, Berber, and North African music. The frequent use of 1.5 steps in the scale helps create a sound which is commonly associated with a lot of Middle Eastern music. The oud is the most popular stringed instrument used in Andalusian classical music. It is a pear-shaped, stringed instrument and is distinguished by its absence of frets. It originally had four strings, but today may have five or six. It is the ancestor of all lutes and even the guitar. The oud is probably of Persian origin and was refined during the Arab golden age.

SOME G ALGERIAN SCALE SHAPES

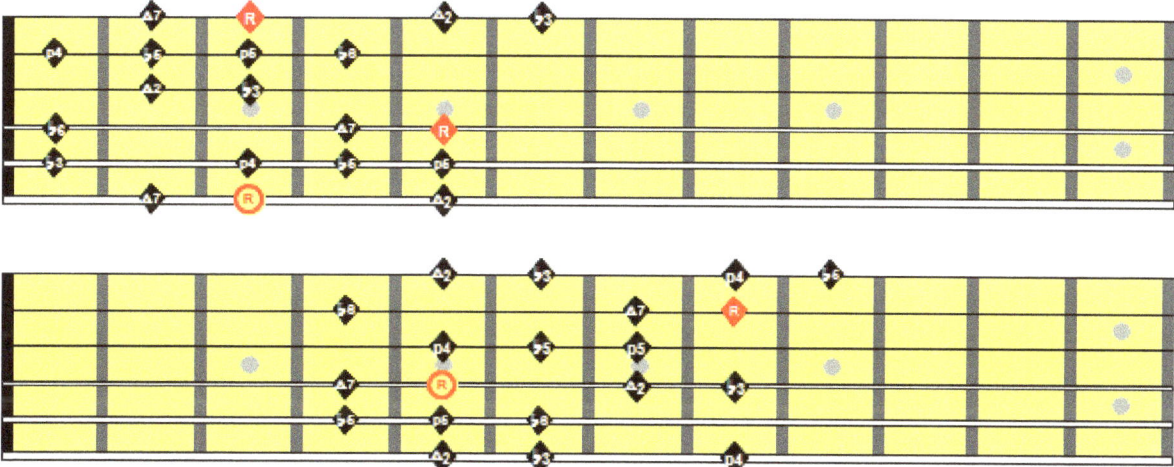

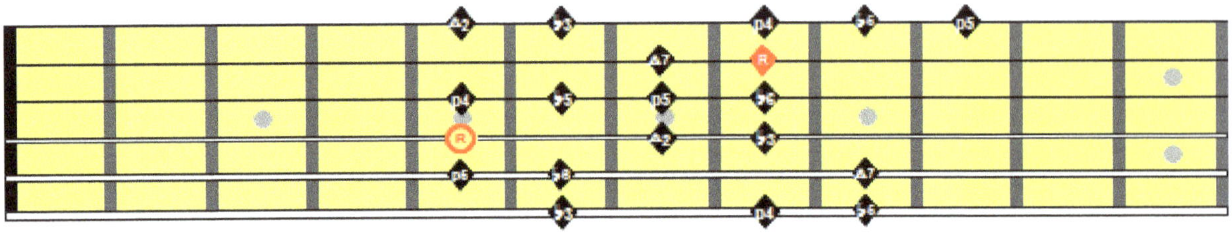

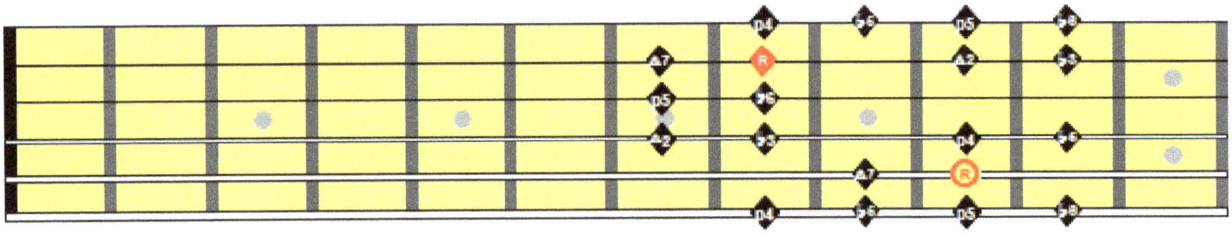

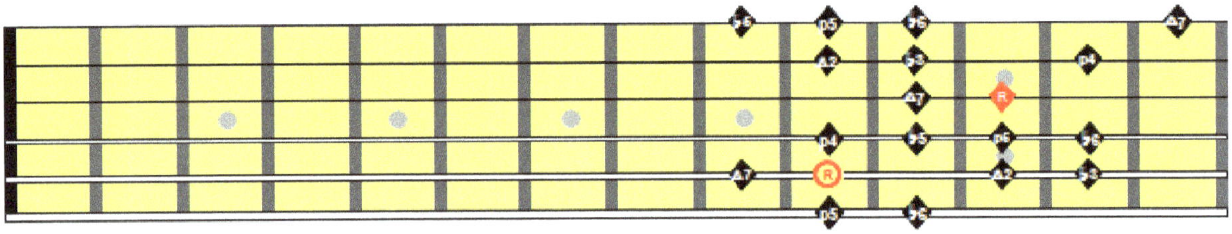

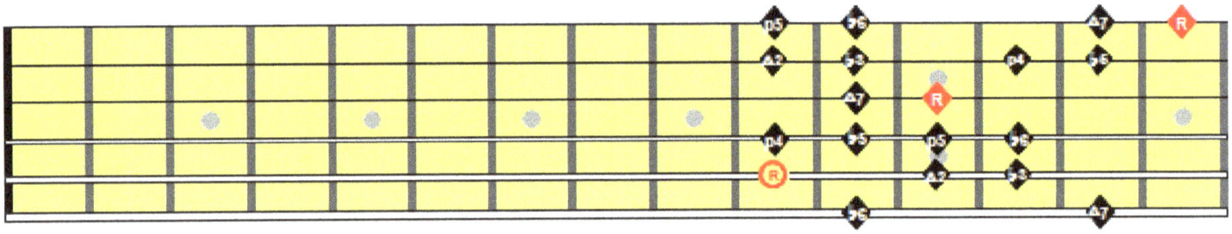

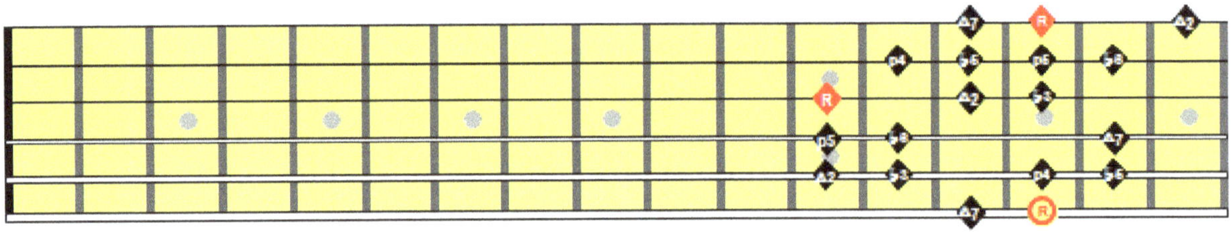

SOME CHORDS FORMED FROM THE G ALGERIAN SCALE

G Sus4

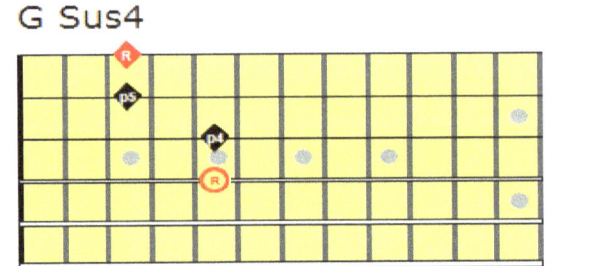

A Diminished

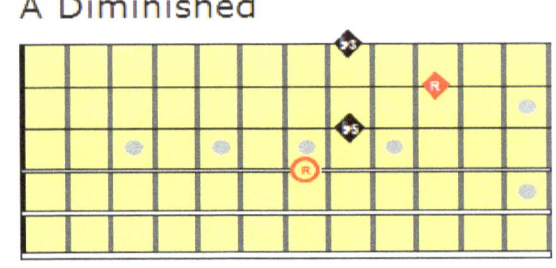

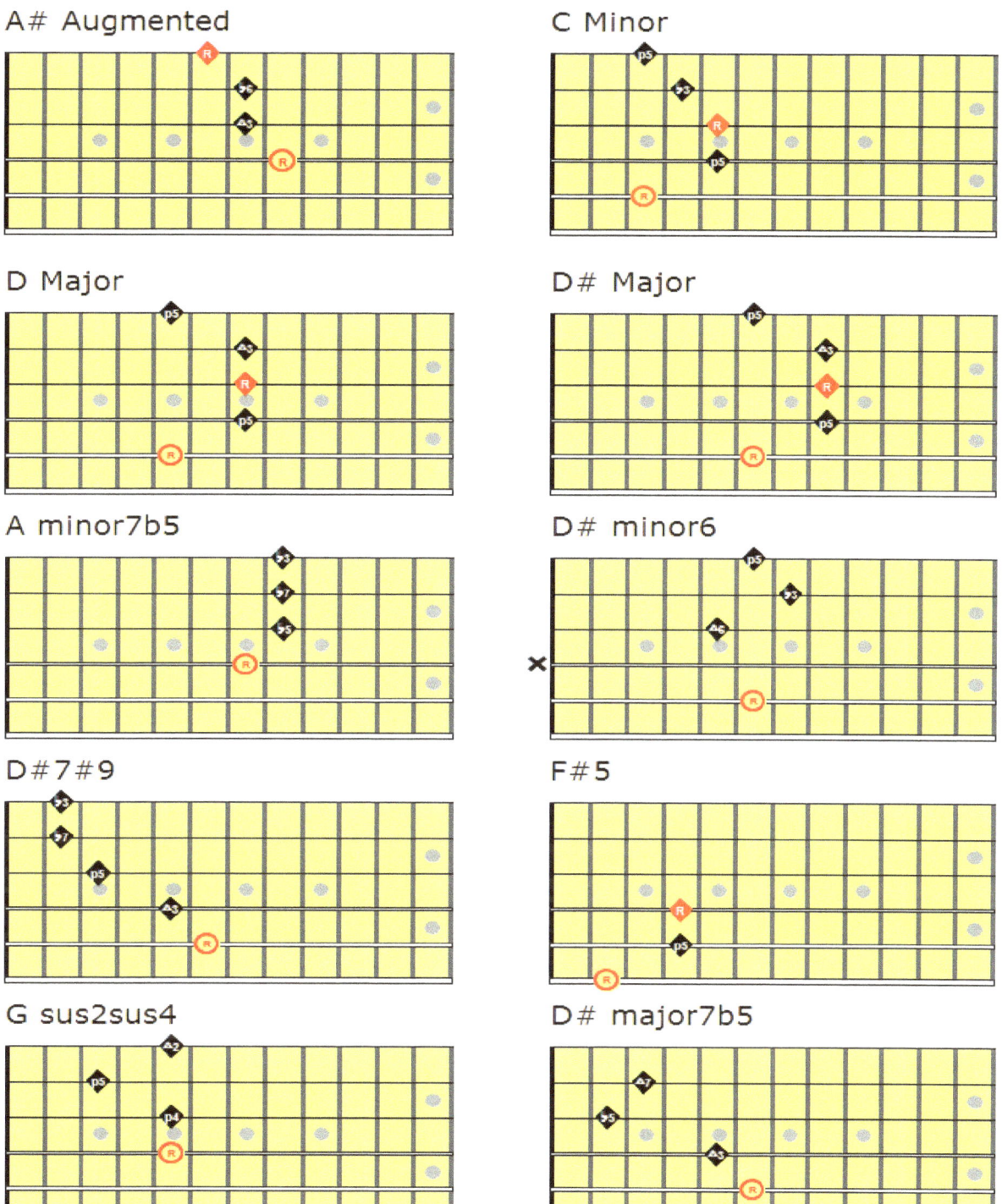

A# Augmented

C Minor

D Major

D# Major

A minor7b5

D# minor6

D#7#9

F#5

G sus2sus4

D# major7b5

G ALGERIAN SCALE LICKS

Use some economy picking in the first bar. Economy picking is a hybrid of sweep picking and alternate picking. In the second bar string skip and target the **G** note on the 17th fret, fourth string.

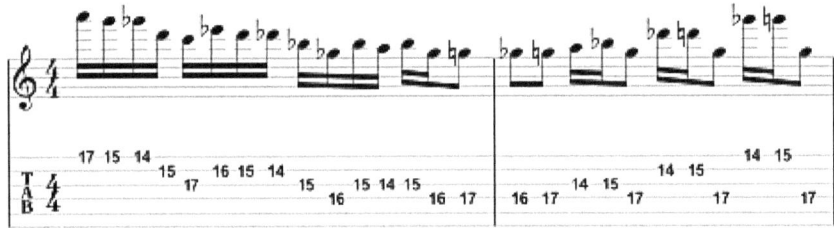

In this lick you play half steps on each string of the guitar. A half step is the smallest interval in Western musical scales. I'm playing over a Gsus4 and a Dsus4 chord.

This next lick is an ascending sequence. Start with the Root (G) and play the first five notes of the scale. Next, play the second note of the scale and ascend five notes—continue this pattern.

This next lick is played using 4ths. Start with the root of the scale and then play the 4th note of the scale. Then, go to the second note of the scale and count four notes from there and continue in that pattern.

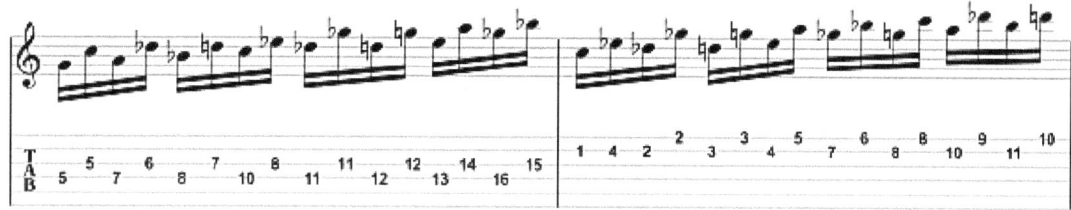

This lick starts out with an octave lick and then goes into a 1/16th note triplet lick and then has some 32nd notes.

This is a melodic lick using the G Algerian scale.

ARABIAN SCALE

Intervals

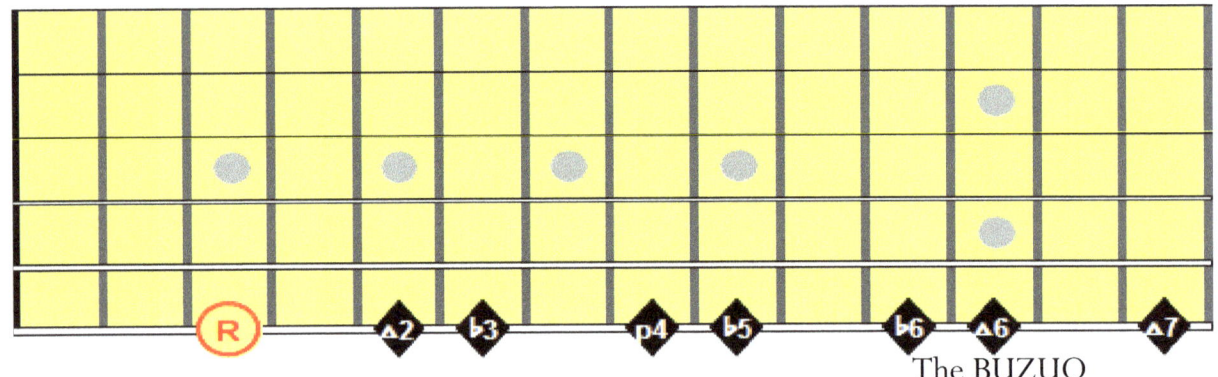

The BUZUQ

Formula: R, 2nd, b3rd, 4th, b5th, b6th, 6th, 7th

IN STEPS: W H W H W H W

SOME INTERESTING ARABIAN INSTRUMENTS

The BUZUQ

The buzuq is slightly limited for the execution of the Arabic maqam, given that it's fretted. However frets are usually added for the most common quarter tones (Eb, Ab and Bb), and can be moved for additional fine tuning. Despite that fact a slight difference in intonation is noticed when the buzuq plays alongside a oud or a qanun for example

The word buzuq is Turkish and occurs in 'bashi-buzuq,' the name given to the Ottoman troops, literally meaning 'burnt head' or 'uprooted.' In its folk form, the buzuq is a larger and deeper-toned relative of the Turkish saz and has a body carved from a single piece of wood. In its modern, urbanized form, the body is constructed from separate ribs and has mechanical, rather than wooden pegs.

A long-necked fretted lute, the buzuq is usually furnished with two courses of metal strings, a double (C4) and a triple (G3), played with a thin piece of horn or a plastic plectrum. The metal strings give the instrument a bright sound quality, while the fret distribution (~24 movable frets) offers many microtonal possibilities.

The buzuq, typically used as a solo instrument, is not considered a member of the standard Arab ensemble. It is found in both folk and urban contexts in Syria, Lebanon, Palestine and Jordan, and is associated with itinerant Gypsy musicians. The Rahbanis (Lebanon) latety popularized the use of this instrument and made it more mainstream.

The VIOLIN

The European violin (also called **Kaman/Kamanjah** in Arabic) was adopted into Arab music during the second half of the 19th century, replacing an indigenous two-string fiddle that was prevalent in Egypt also called kamanjah. Although various tunings are used, the traditional Arab tuning is in fourths and fifths (G3, D4, G4, D5.) As a fretless instrument the violin can produce all shades of intonation of the Arabic maqam.

The playing style is highly ornate, with slides, trills, wide vibrato, and double stops, often using an open string as a drone. The timbre ranges from rich and warm, similar to the sound of the Western violin, to nasal and penetrating, reminiscent of the sound of the rababah, a type of Arab folk fiddle.

The violin is held both in the usual under-chin fashion and gamba style on the knee. Moroccans play gamba style and often Moroccans use the GDAE tuning.

SOME HISTORY OF ARABIAN MUSIC

The account of Arabic music can be separated into numerous central periods. The earliest is the pre-Islamic era—the epoch of Jahiliyyah—ignorance, as it is called. This expression, of course, was coined by the Muslim thinkers of later periods. All the information we have about the music of this time, which is described as uncomplicated and archaic, is from those thinkers of the 9th century and later. During the Jahiliyyah era music was most likely comprised of songs of wandering and journeys, in which the lyrics were more important than the melody. It is known that there was already contact with bordering cultures such as the Babylonian kingdom and the Assyrian realm, which flourished in the region at the time. The wandering tribes also passed cultural messages to and from adjacent societies.

The Arabian scale is an eight tone scale. The Arabian scale is an octatonic minor scale (it has 8 notes). It is the same scale as the diminished scale.

Some of the fretted instruments used in Arabian music include the Buzuq. A buzuq is a long-necked fretted lute. Another instrument used is called a Guembri, which is a three stringed skin-covered bass plucked lute.

SOME G ARABIAN SCALE SHAPES

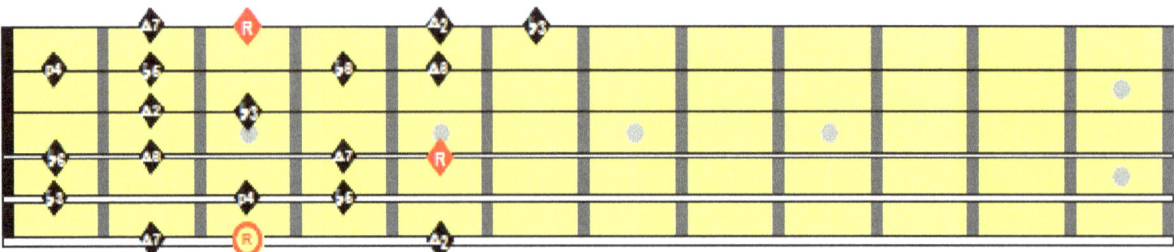

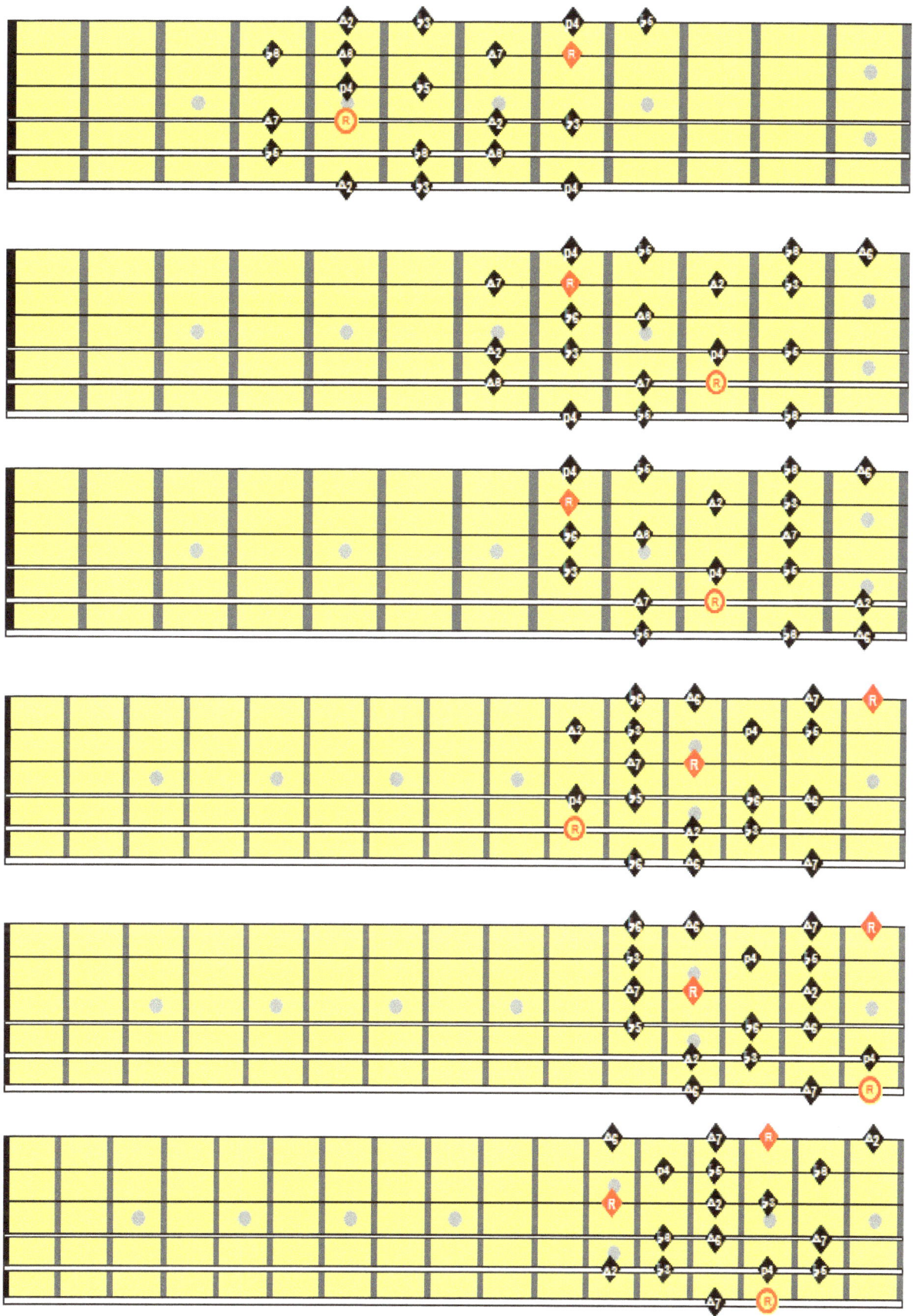

SOME CHORDS FORMED FROM THE G ARABIAN SCALE

G Diminished

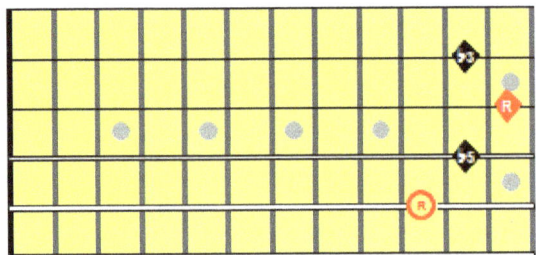

A Major

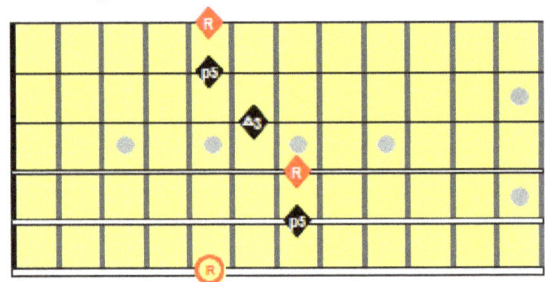

A# Diminished

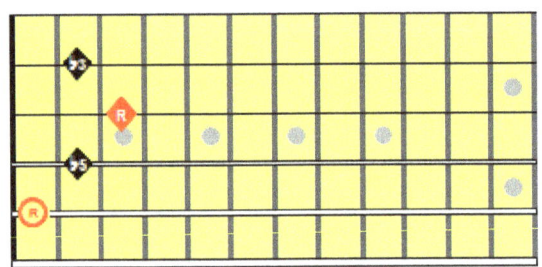

C Major

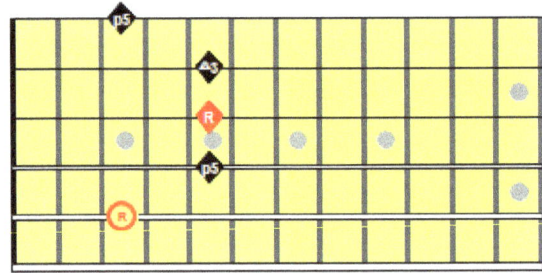

C# Diminished

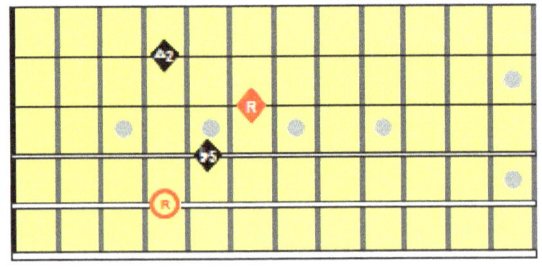

D Major

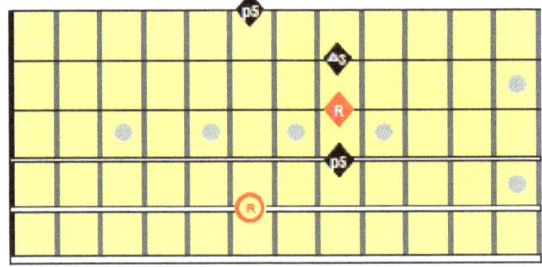

D#6

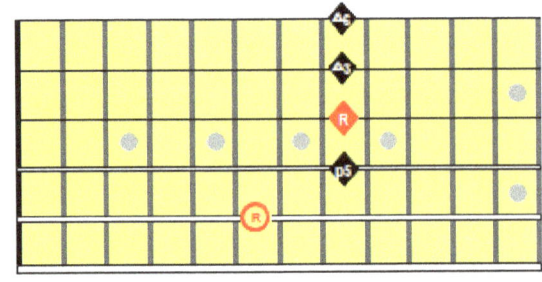

A6

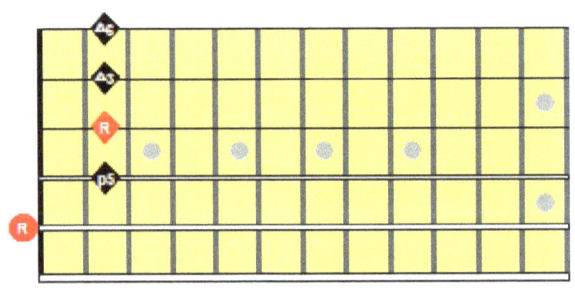

G diminished7

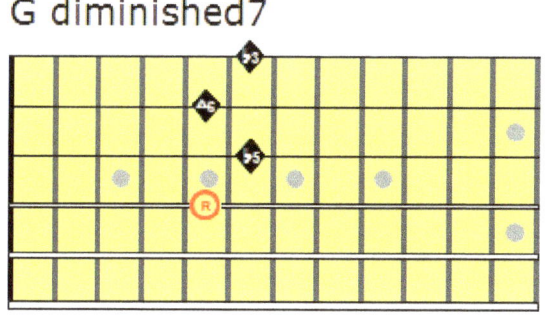

F#Major

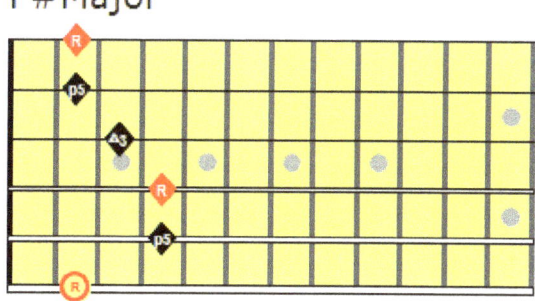

C minor7b5

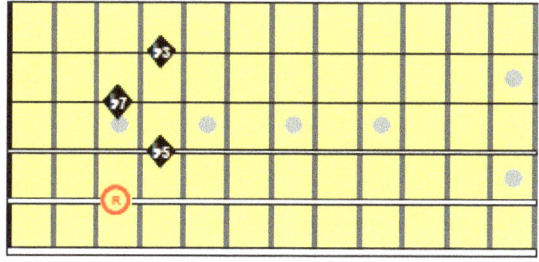

A5

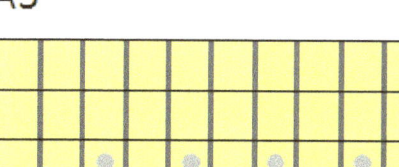

G ARABIAN SCALE LICKS

This is an ascending lick using the Arabian scale with some sequencing in the second bar. This is played over Edim7—Gdim7

In the lick below you can use 4ths to make a cool double stop lick/riff.

This next lick has some 1/16 note triplets. In bar two, you can do an interesting intervallic lick.

In this lick you play a pattern where you play three notes on the high E string, then play one note on the B string and one on the G string. Then, do the same pattern, but this time start on the second string.

BYZANTINE SCALE

Intervals

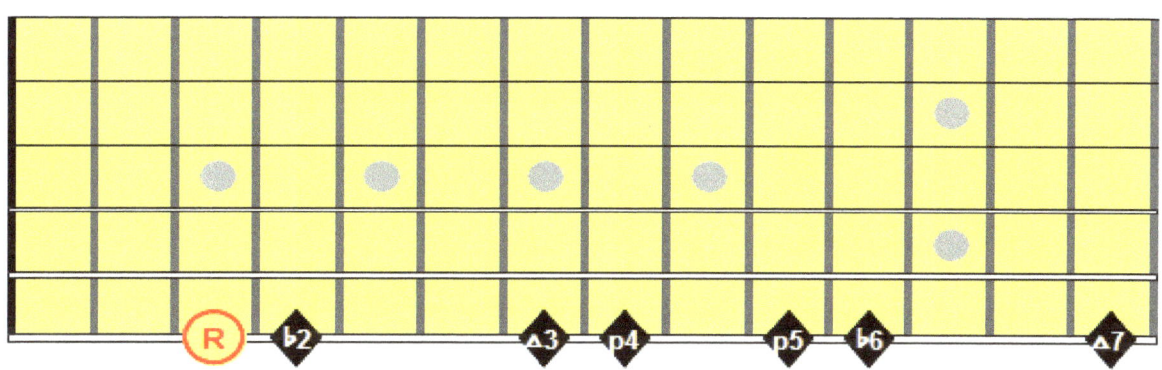

Formula: R, b2nd, 3rd, 4th, 5th, b6th, 7th

IN STEPS: H W + H H W H W + H

In music, the double harmonic major scale is a scale with gaps that evoke "exotic" music to Western listeners. This is also known as the Gypsy, Arabic and the Byzantine scale. The double harmonic scale is uncommonly used in Western music, as it does not closely follow any of the basic musical modes, nor is it easily derived from them. It also does not easily fit into common Western chord progressions such as the authentic cadence.

STRINGED BYZANTINE INSTRUMENTS

A Lyra is a stringed instrument of the harp class having an approximately U-shaped frame and used by the ancient Greeks especially to accompany song and recitation. The LYRA of the Greeks of Pontos (Black Sea region of Asia Minor) is also known as the Kementse. It is played like a violin (violi) with a primitive style bow, but the musicians hold the lyra in an upright position. Sometimes they rest the instrument on their knee when they are sitting, and sometimes it is held out in front of them. They sometimes even dance in front of the dancers while holding the lyra in that way.

The LYRA

The **tzouras** is a long necked string instrument which is in the bouzouki family of instruments. The tzouras is also called a tambouras, and is similar to the ancient and Byzantine forms of the long necked stringed instruments. The body of the tzouras is smaller than that of a bouzouki.

A drawing of the TZOURAS

The **bouzouki** is the main or lead folk instrument found in the taverna style or rebetiki music of the seaports and urban areas of Greece. The bouzouki is the descendent of ancient Greek and eastern instruments. In ancient times the name of this long-necked string instrument was the "trichordo" or "three stringed instrument."

The BOUZOUKI

SOME HISTORY OF BYZANTINE MUSIC

Long considered to be merely an additional expansion of early Greek music, Byzantine music is now regarded as a sovereign melodic culture, with rudiments derived from Syrian and Hebrew as well as Greek sources. Its early development has been dated by some scholars to the 4th century, after the origin of the Eastern kingdom by Constantine I.

SOME G BYZANTINE SCALE SHAPES

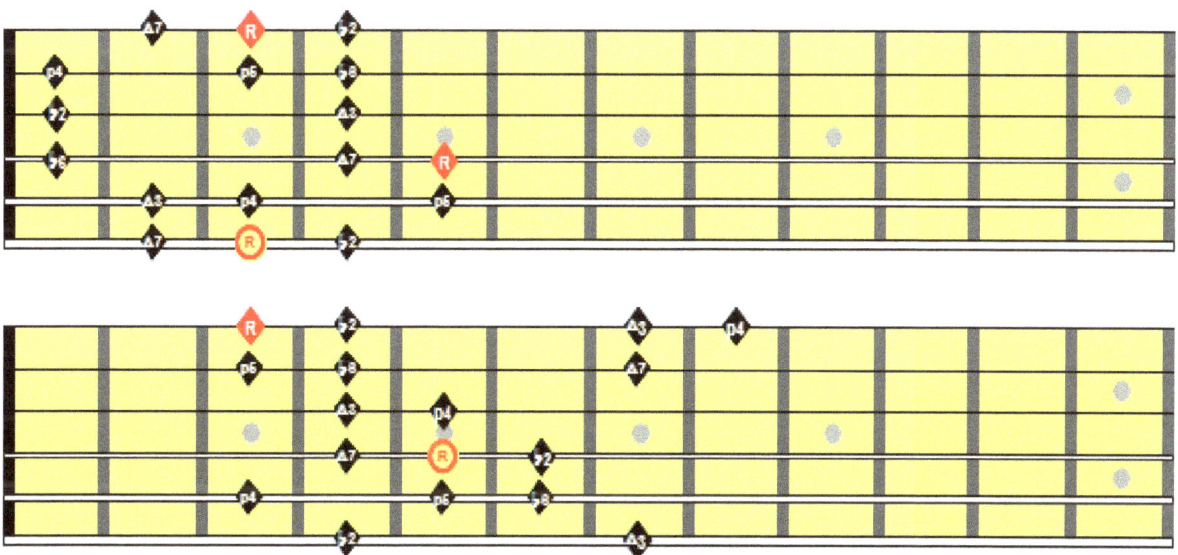

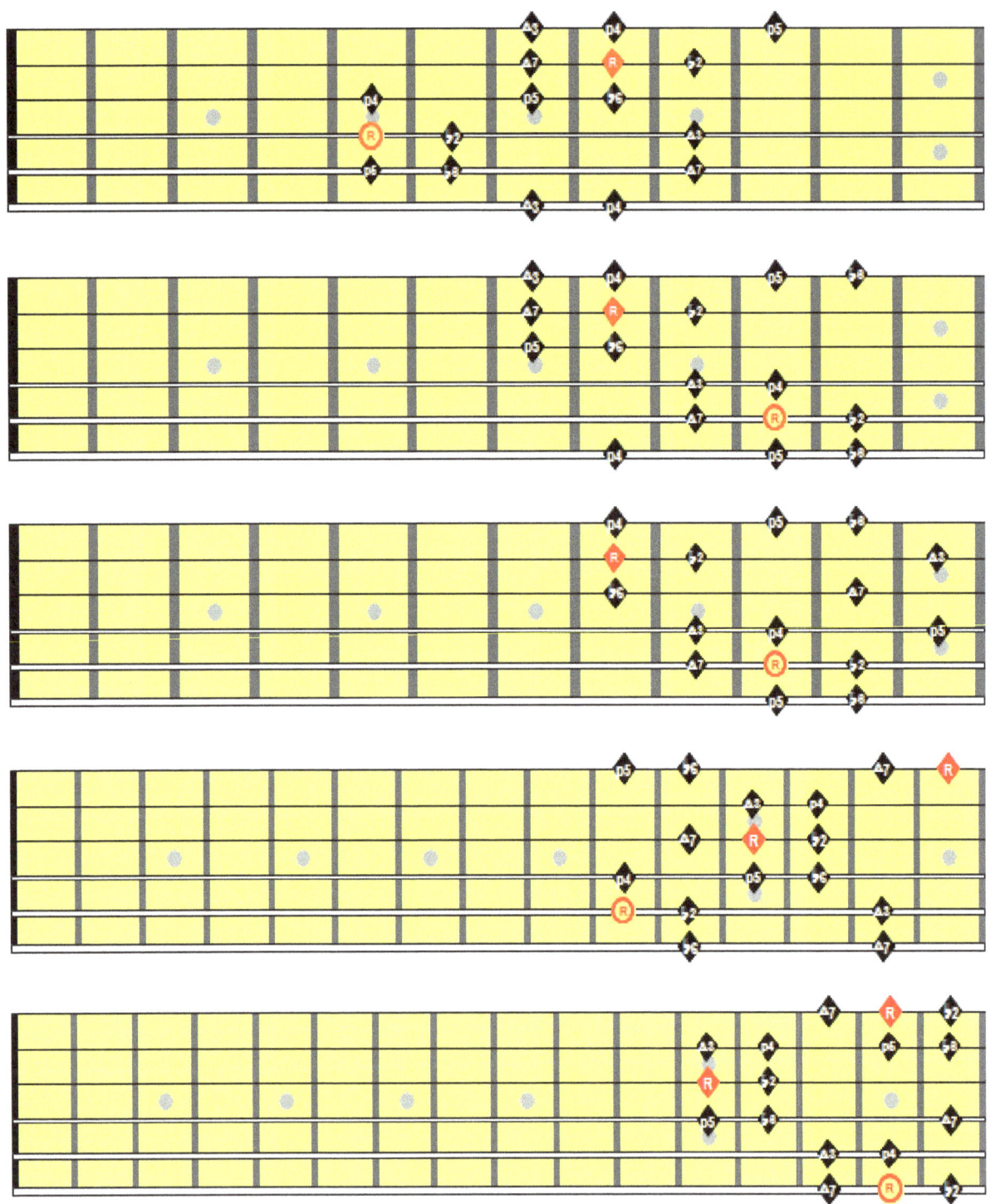

SOME CHORDS FORMED FROM THE G BYZANTINE SCALE

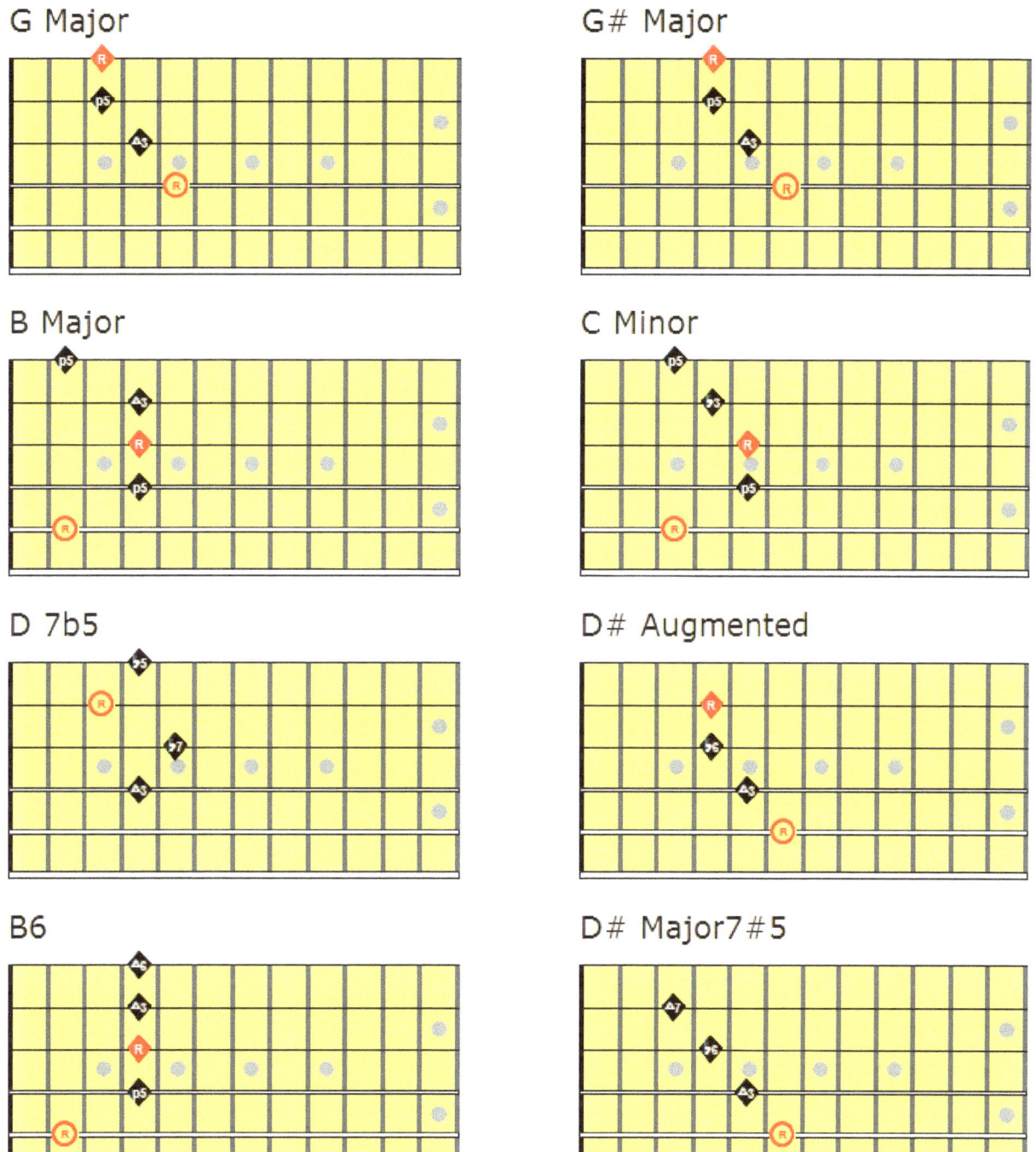

G Major

G# Major

B Major

C Minor

D 7b5

D# Augmented

B6

D# Major7#5

G#Major7b5

C Sus2

G Sus4

B5

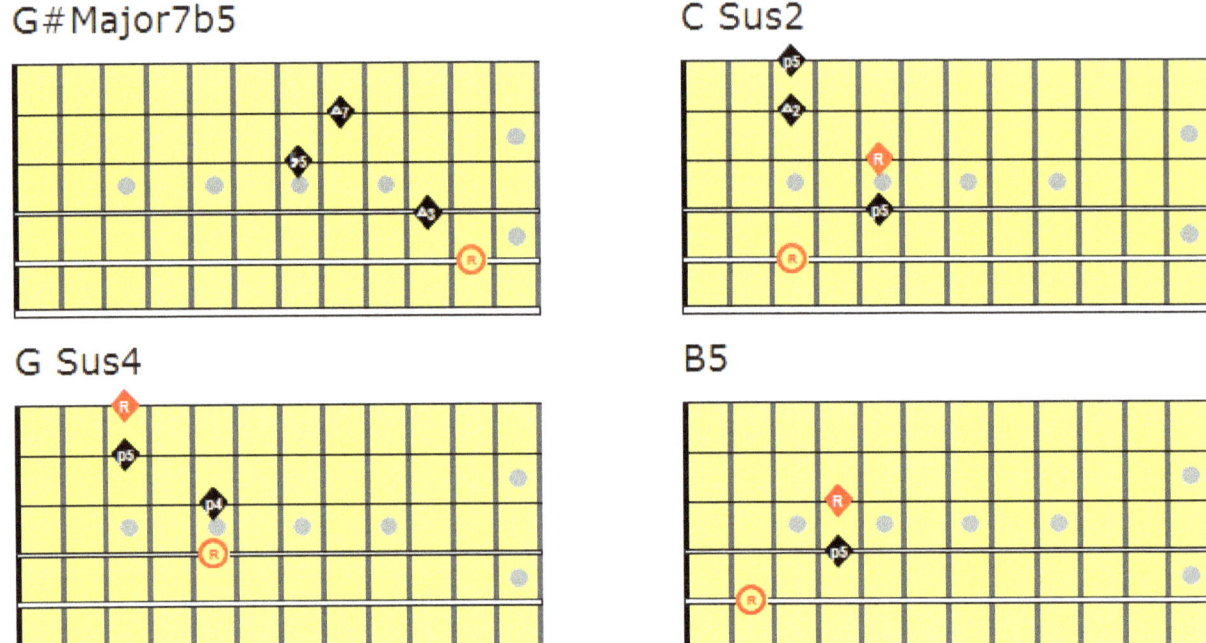

G BYZANTINE SCALE LICKS

Bars one and two have a cool string skipping lick from the second string to the fourth string. Bar three is an ascending lick. Bar four is a descending lick, and Bar five is played using octaves.

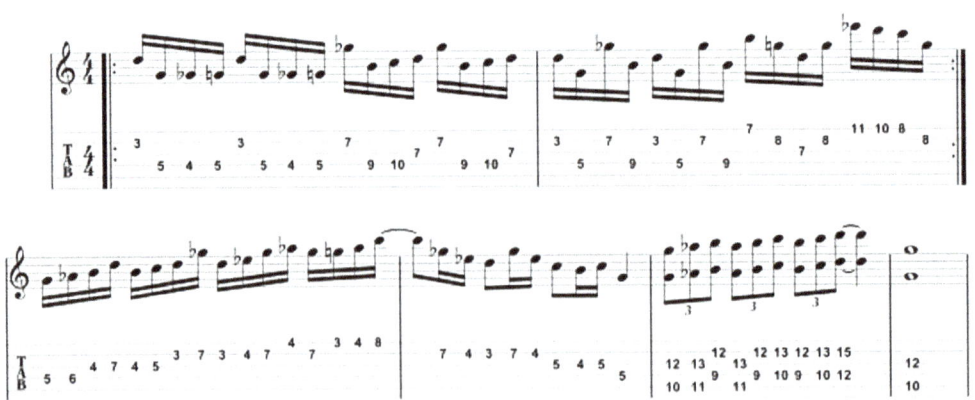

This next lick is played in all octaves with vibrato. It has an eerie horror flick kind of sound.

In this next lick, you can play arpeggios. The arpeggios you'll play here are: B minor, D# augmented, G maj7, G# diminished, C minor, G Sus4, G# minor 7, C Sus2

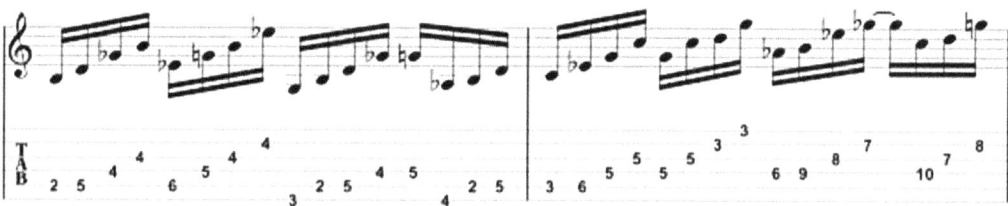

This lick has an interesting haunting melody using the G Byzantine scale.

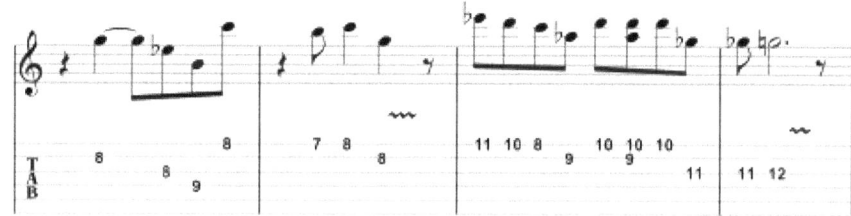

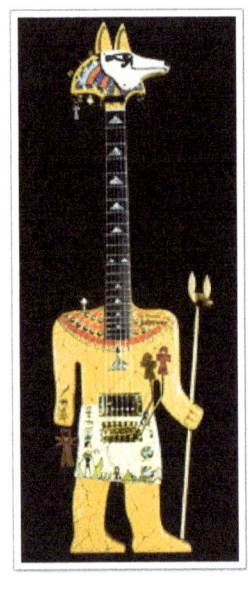

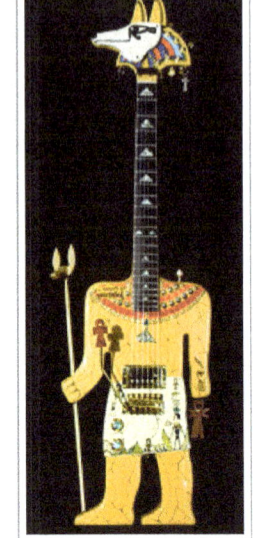

EGYPTIAN SCALE

Intervals

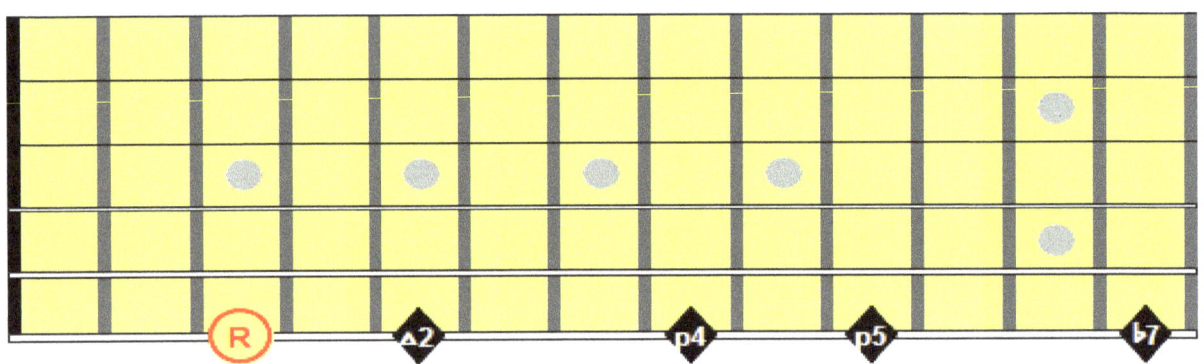

Formula: R, 2ⁿᵈ, 4ᵗʰ, 5ᵗʰ, b7th

IN STEPS: W W + H W W + H

> **The Egyptian scale is a five tone scale. A five tone scale is also referred to as a pentatonic scale.**

SOME HISTORY OF EGYPTIAN MUSIC

Music found its way into numerous contexts in Egypt: temples, palaces, workshops, farms, battlefields and the tomb. Music was an integral part of sacred worship in early Egypt, so it is not startling that there were gods particularly connected with music, such as Hathor and Bes.

The KANUN

In Egypt a **Kanun** is a type of large zither with a narrow trapezoidal soundboard. Nylon or PVC strings are stretched over a single bridge poised on fish-skins on one end, attached to tuning pegs at the other end.

SOME G EGYPTIAN SCALE SHAPES

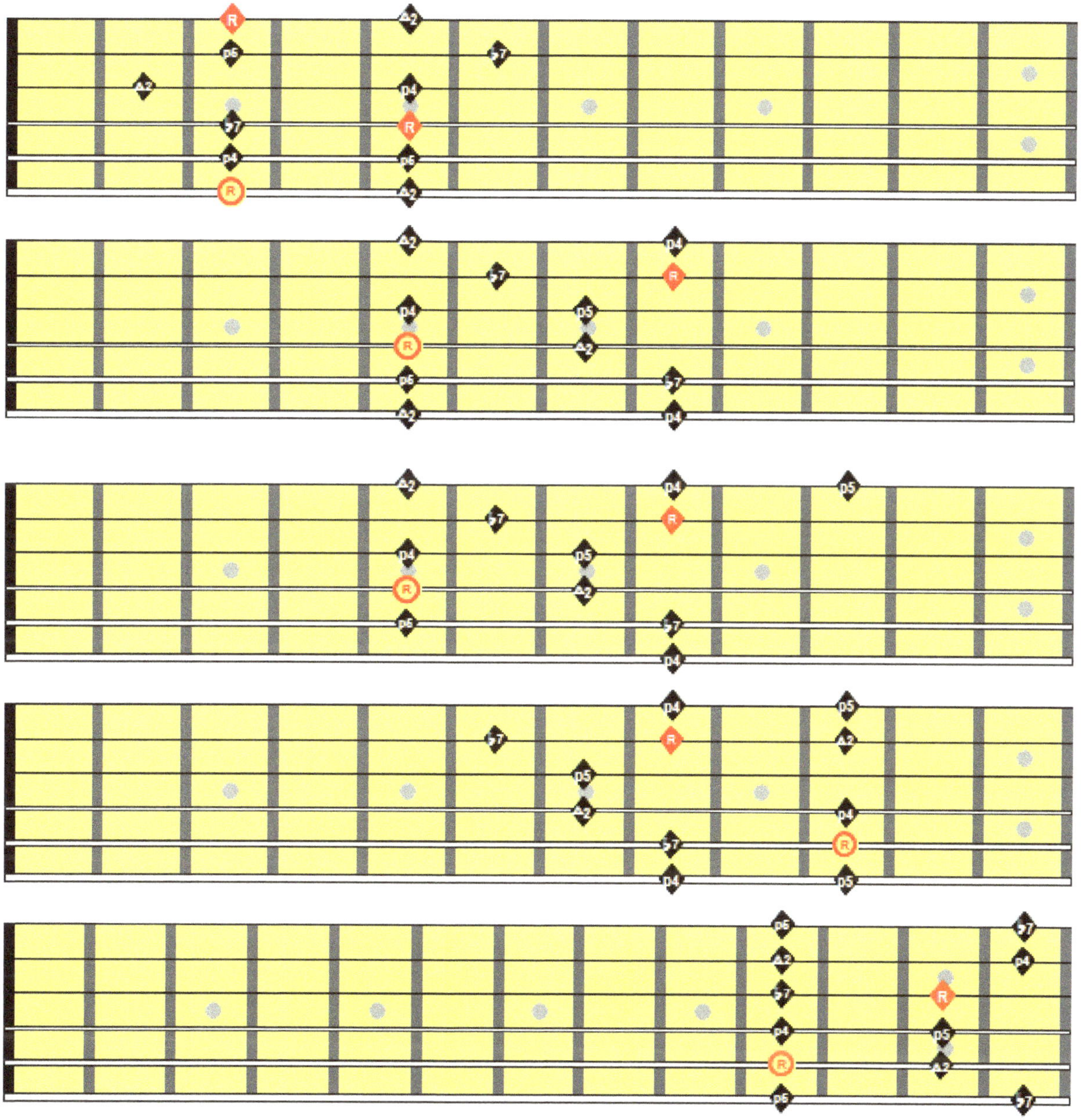

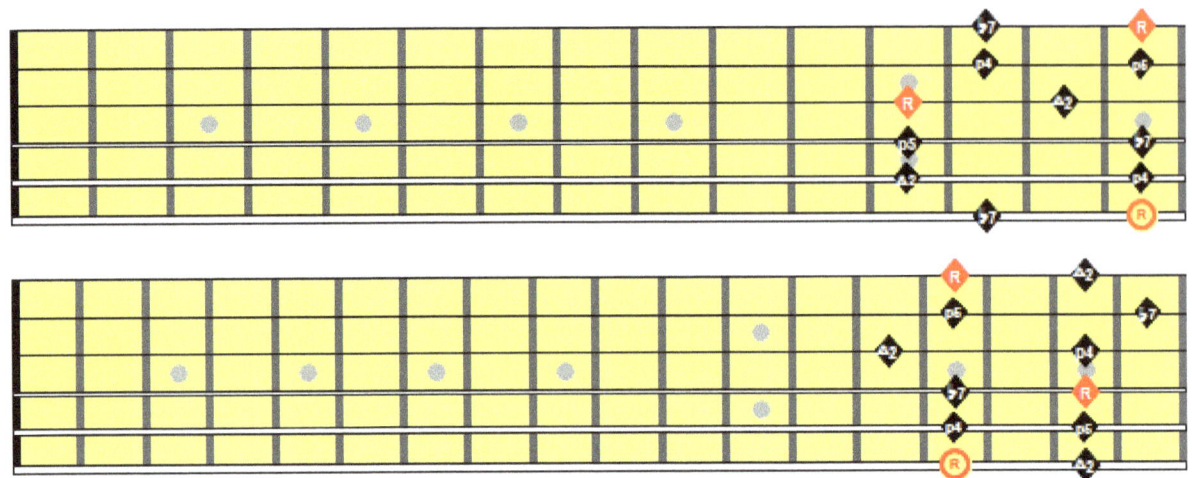

SOME CHORDS FORMED FROM THE G EGYPTIAN SCALE

G Sus4

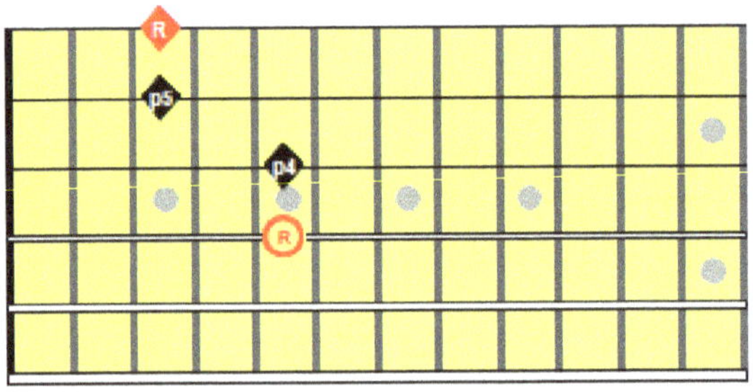

C Sus2

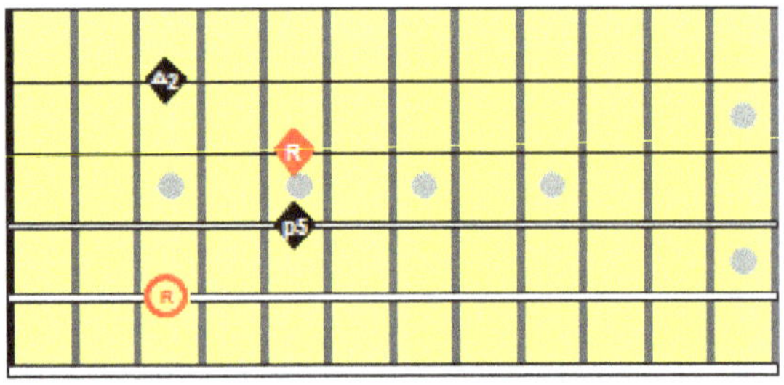

A min7#5

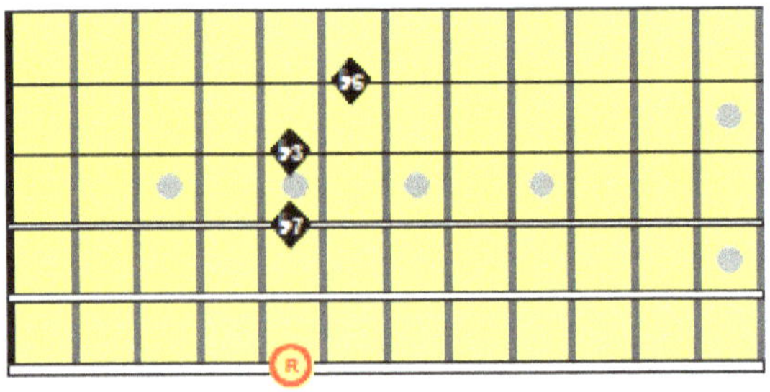

F Sus2

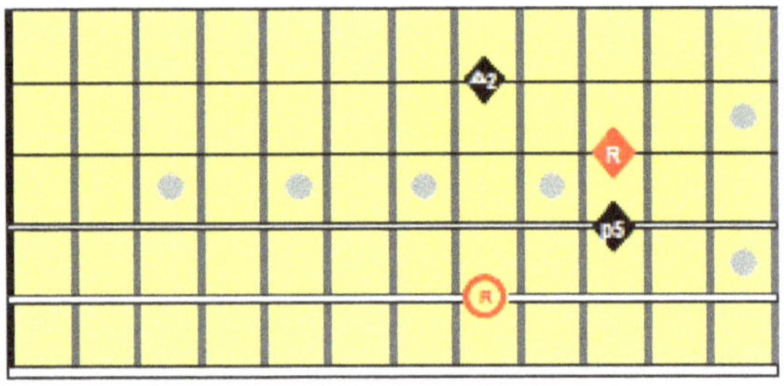

D min7

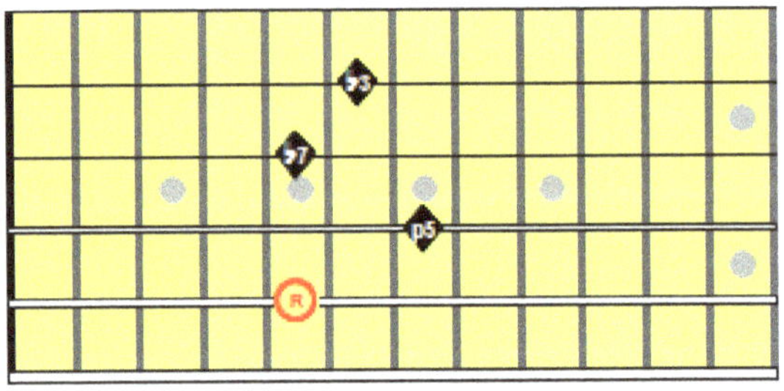

D7Sus4

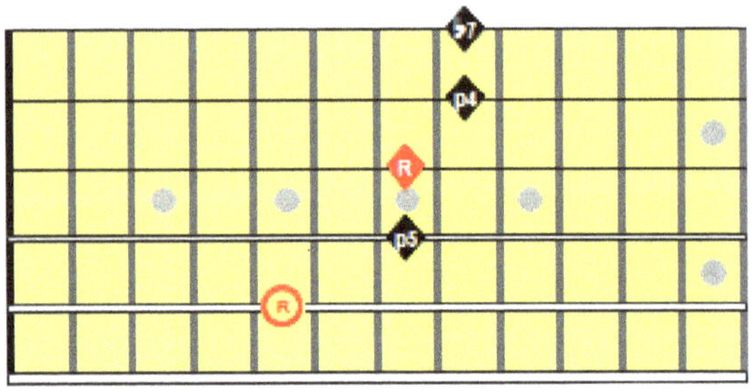

A minor7#5

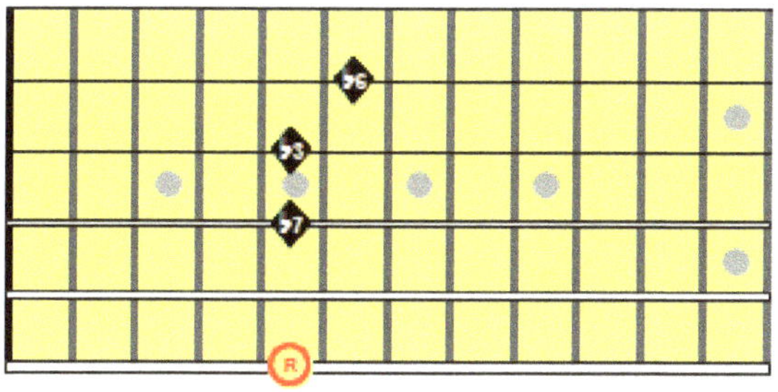

G5

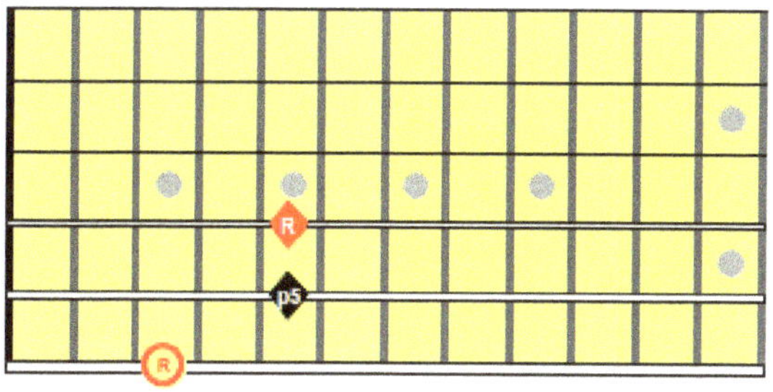

G Sus2Sus4

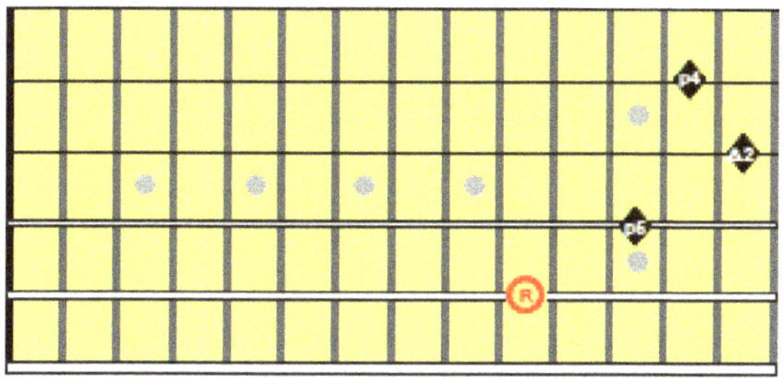

F5

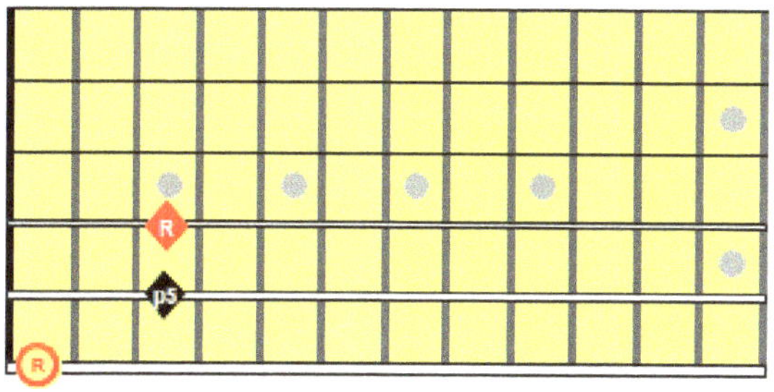

F Major

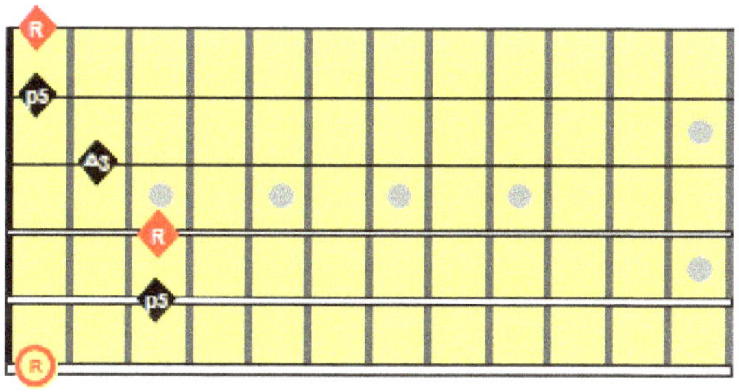

D5

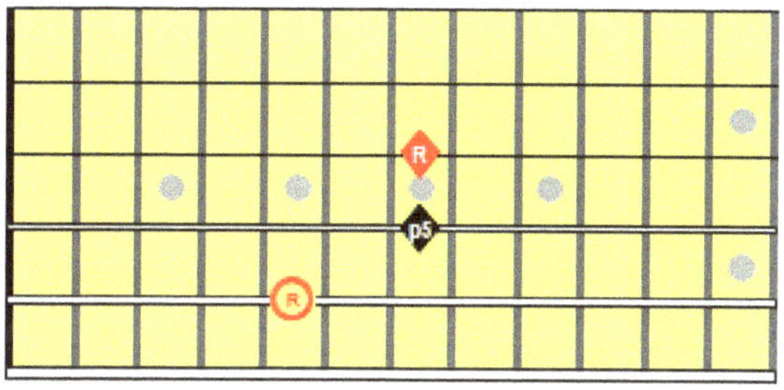

Bar one has some 1/8 note triplets. Bar two and three have some double stops. Bars three and four have some arpeggios.

G EGYPTIAN SCALE LICKS

This next lick has some slides. This lick ascends and then descends in a reverse pattern. (I really lick this lick.)

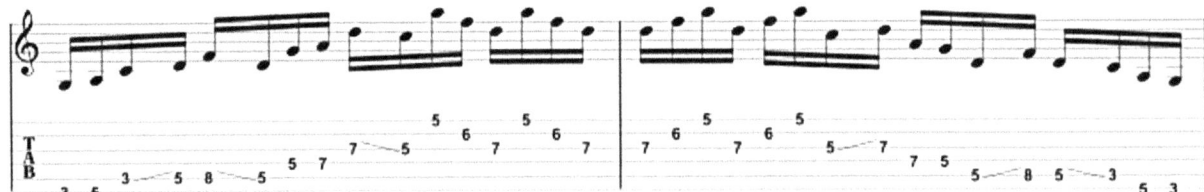

This is a melodic riff over and F Major Arpeggio and a G Sus4 arpeggio.

This next lick has some awesome slides and octaves.

EIGHT-TONE SPANISH SCALE

Intervals

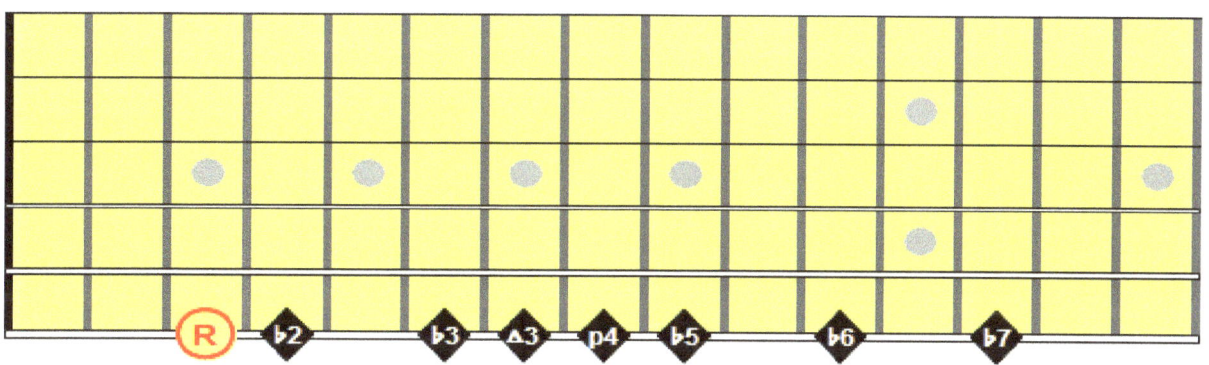

Formula: R, b2nd, b3rd, 3rd, 4th, b5th, b6th, b7th

IN STEPS: H W H H H W W W

SOME HISTORY OF SPANISH MUSIC

During the initial eras of Spain's existence, meshing cultures unintentionally impacted each other on every stage—and without a doubt contributed considerably to the account of Spanish music.

The history of Spanish music continued to develop with the birth of the Renaissance period. Instrumental music emerged and flourished, most notably with the influence of Arabic music and the development of the Spanish guitar.

39

SOME G EIGHT-TONE SPANISH SCALE SHAPES

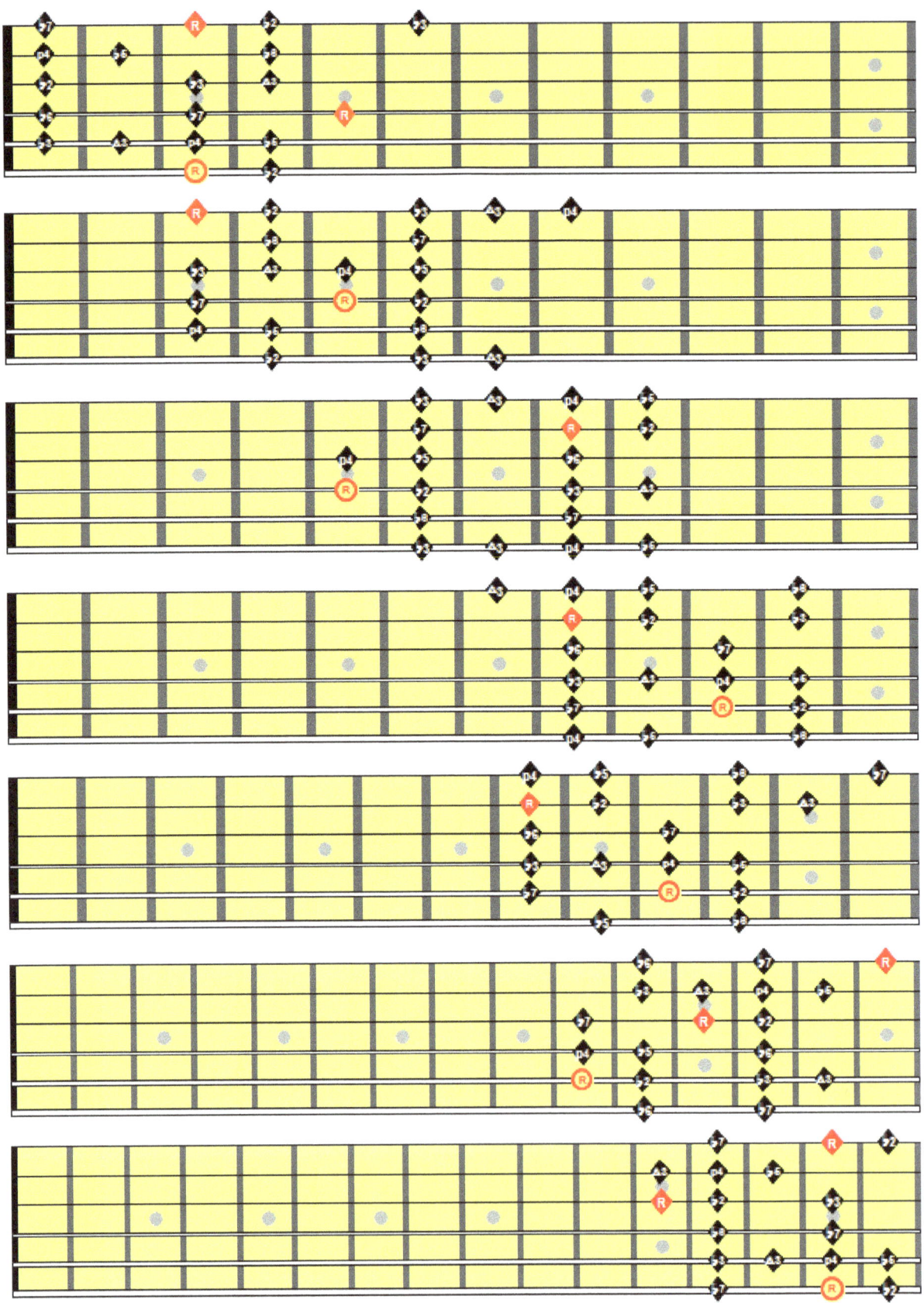

SOME CHORDS FORMED FROM THE G EIGHT-TONE SPANISH SCALE

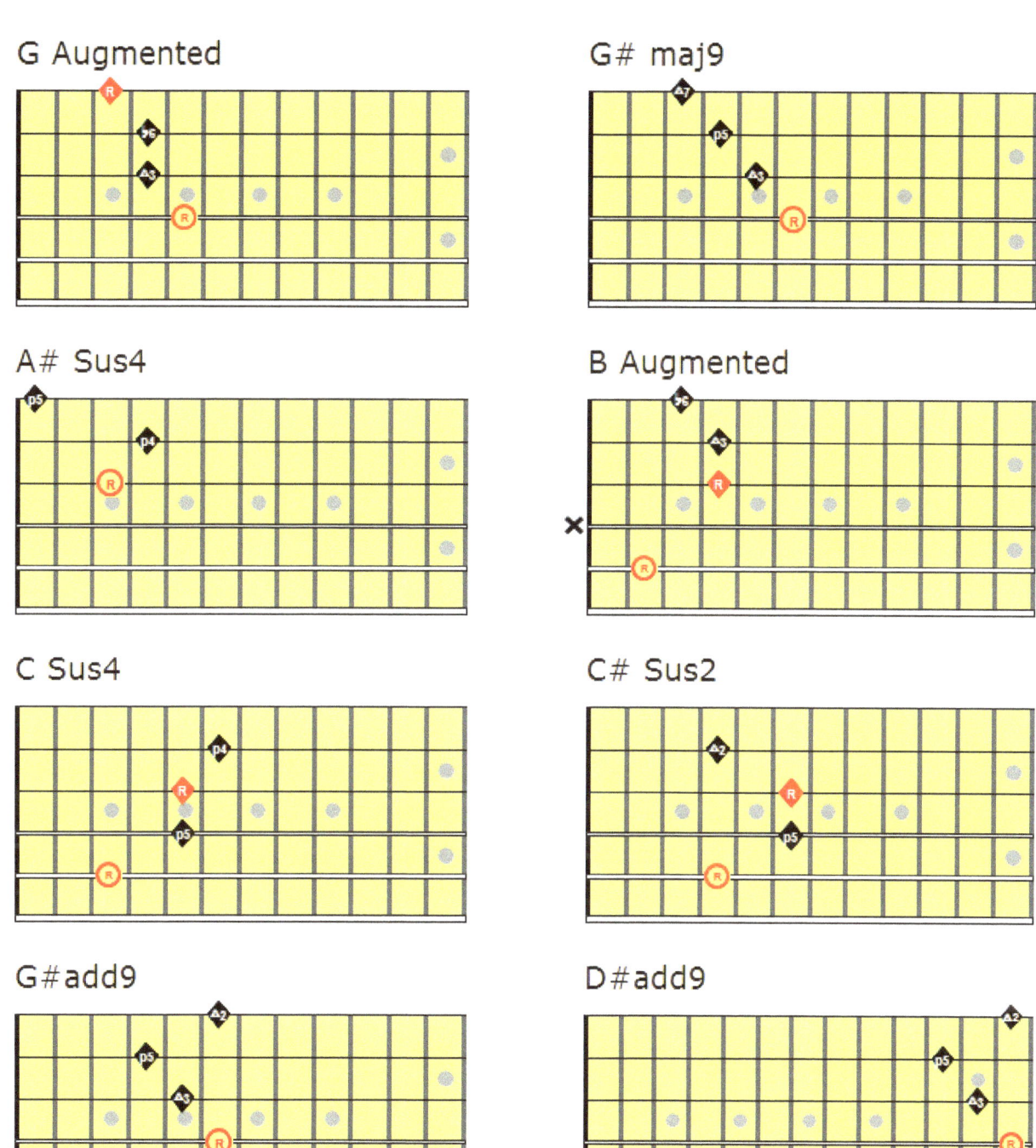

C#7

G Diminished

A#minor7

D#7

G EIGHT-TONE SPANISH SCALE LICKS

This is an interesting lick with some intevallic aspects that make it sound unique.

In this next lick you will be playing 3rds. For example, start at the root of the scale. From there, go to the third note of the scale. Then, go on to the second note of the scale and from there play the fourth note of the scale. The intervals of the scale are: 1, b2, #2, 3, 4, b5, b6, b7

(1,#2) (b2,3) (#2,4) (3,b5) ....You can see what I imply.

I'm using vibrato in this G eight-tone-Spanish scale lick.

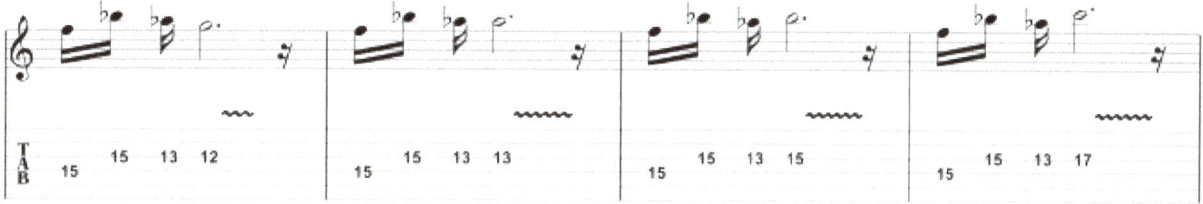

The SPANISH GUITAR

ENIGMATIC SCALE

Intervals

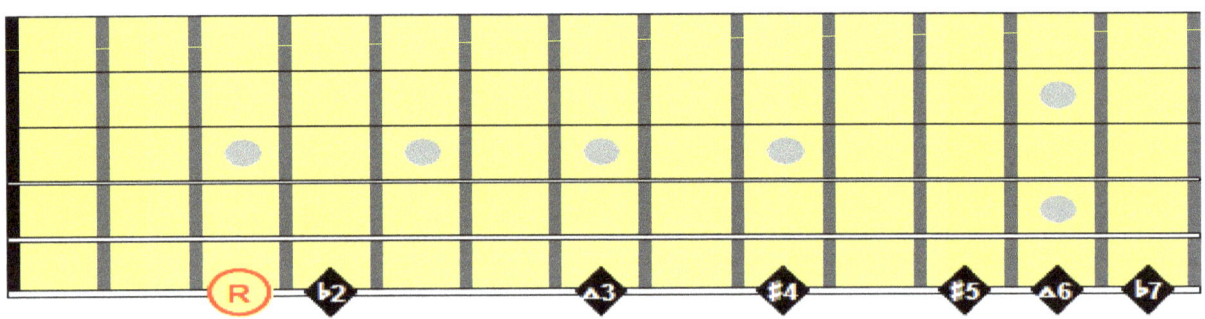

IN STEPS: H W + H W W H H

SOME HISTORY ABOUT THE ENIGMATIC SCALE

The Enigmatic scale was first in print in a Milan paper as a musical test, with an invitation to harmonize it in some way. The Italian musician Giuseppe Verdi allegedly invented the scale.

The scale lacks a perfect fourth (except descending) and a perfect fifth above the opening note. Both the fourth and fifth degrees of a scale form the foundation of standard chord progressions, which help establish the tonic. The scale was used by guitarist Joe Satriani in his piece "The Enigmatic" from *Not of This Earth* (1986).

SOME G ENIGMATIC SCALE SHAPES

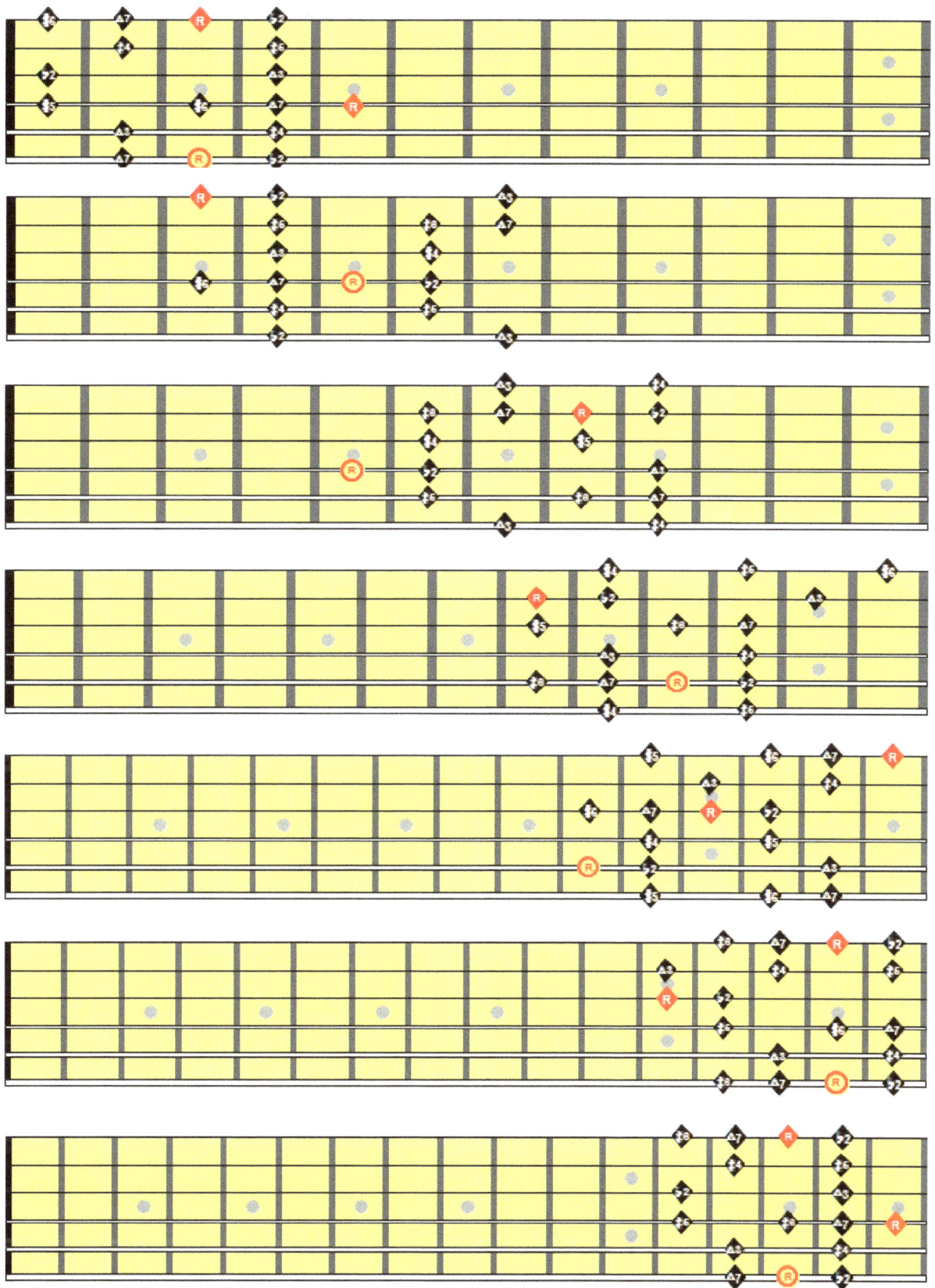

SOME CHORDS FORMED FROM THE G ENIGMATIC SCALE

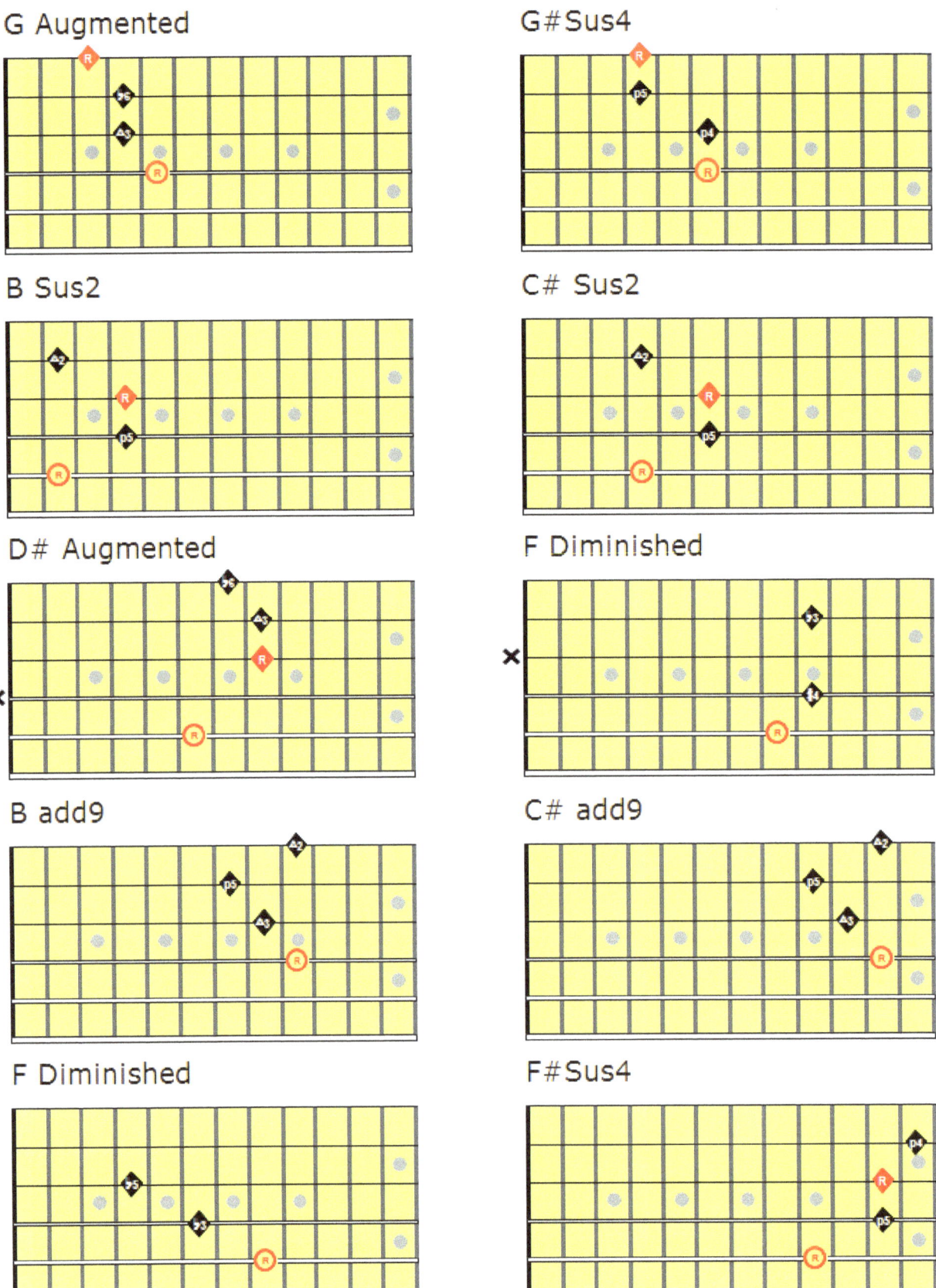

G#Sus4

Bsus2

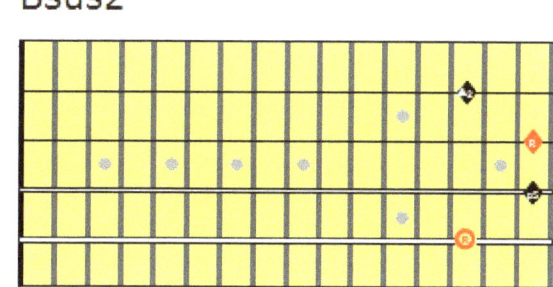

G ENIGMATIC SCALE LICKS

You will be mostly ascending in this lick. Bars two and three have some descending licks.

This next lick is played over a G augmented chord.

This lick is also played over G augmented

HINDUSTAN SCALE

Intervals

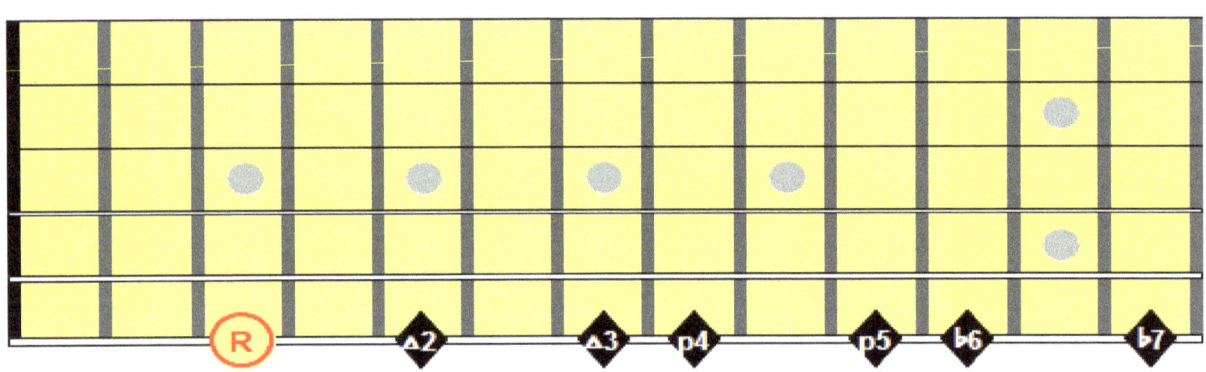

IN STEPS: W W H W H W

Compared to the major scale, the Hindustan scale has a flat 6th and a flat 7th.

STRINGED HINDUSTAN INSTRUMENTS

The *dotar* is a two or four or sometimes five stringed musical instrument resembling more a mandolin than a guitar. It is commonly used in Assam, Bangladesh, West Bengal and Bihar, and dates from the 15th-16th century when it was adopted by the ascetic cults of the Bauls and Fakirs.

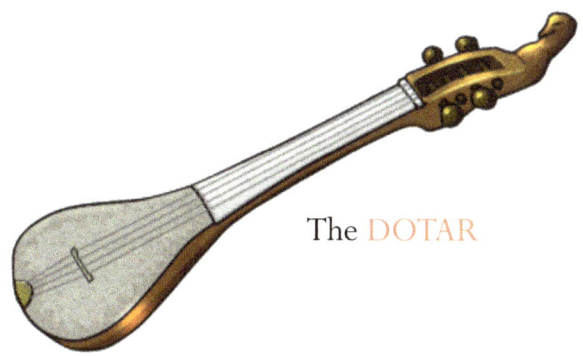

The DOTAR

The **sarod** is a lute like stringed instrument of India, used mainly in Indian classical music. Along with the sitar, it is among the most popular and prominent instruments in Hindustani classical music.

The SAROD

SOME HISTORY OF HINDUSTANI MUSIC

Hindustani music is based on the raga system. A raga is a melodic scale, consisting of notes from the basic seven known as sa, re, ga, ma pa, dha, and ni. Apart from sa and pa which are constant, the other notes may be in major or minor tone, and this gives rise to countless combinations. Ten central scales or thaats are recognized, and other ragas are considered to have evolved from these. A raga must contain a minimum of five notes.

A Sitar is used in Indian music. The sitar is an early Indian musical instrument, which has existed for at least six centuries. The customary acoustic style uses a hollowed-out gourd for the resonating chamber. Unlike most other stringed instruments, the twenty frets are curved and movable, being tied onto the neck.

SOME G HINDUSTAN SCALE SHAPES

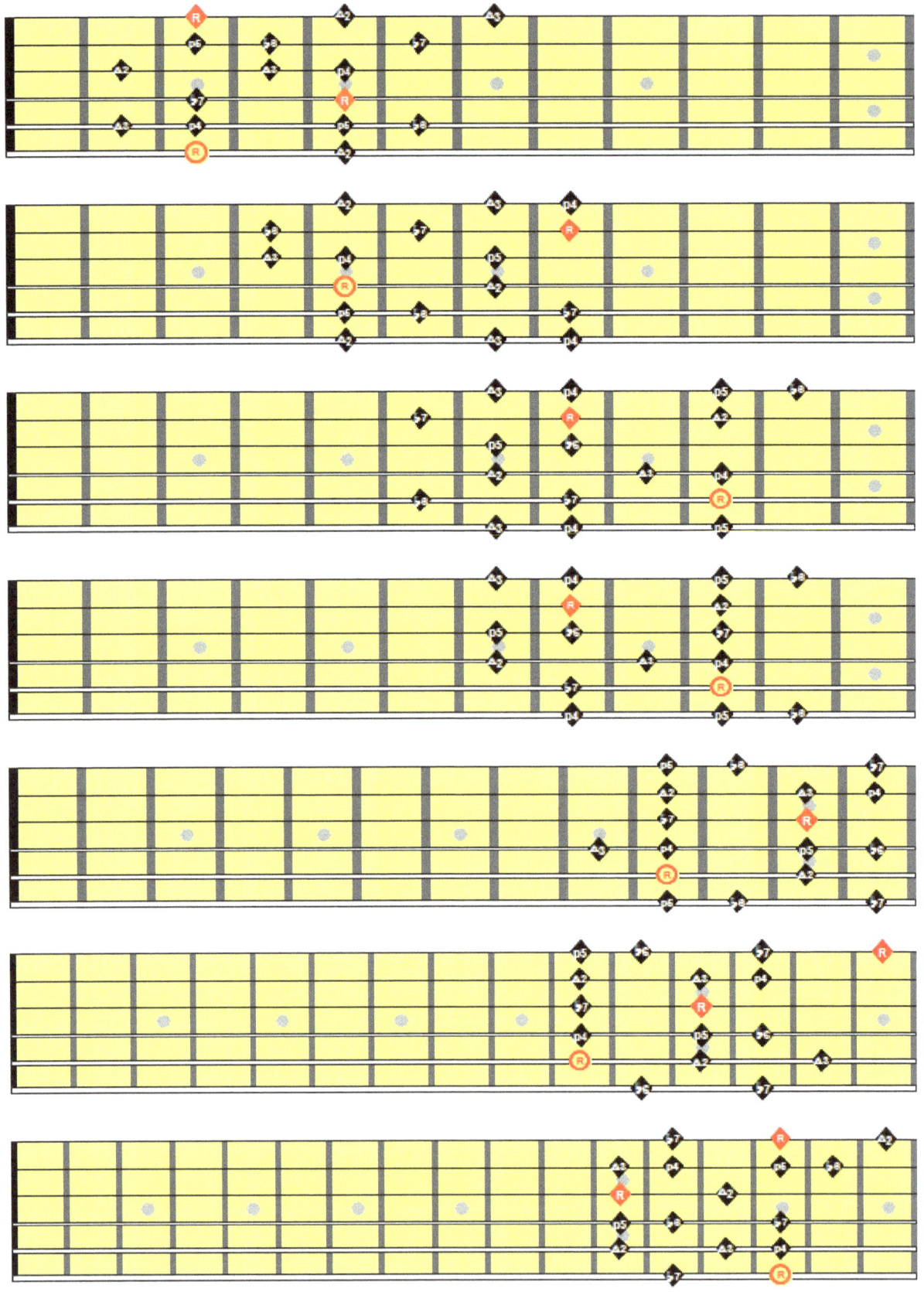

SOME CHORDS FORMED FROM THE G HINDUSTAN SCALE

G Major

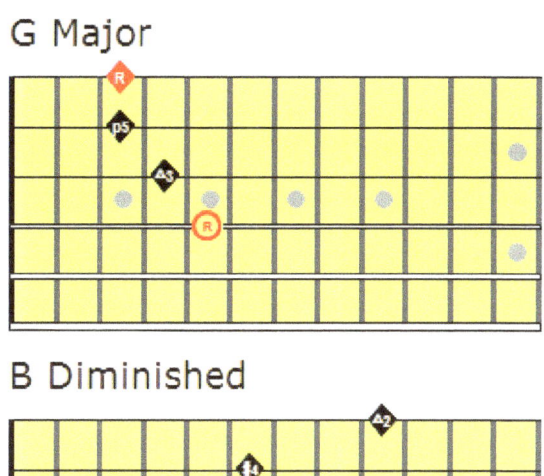

A Diminished

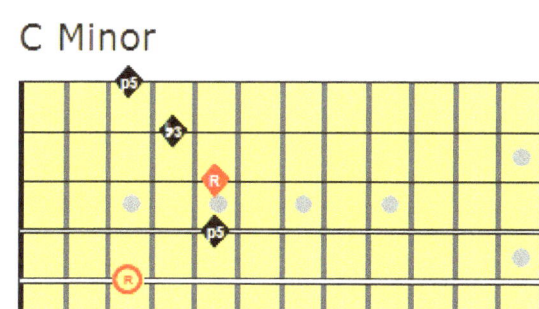

B Diminished

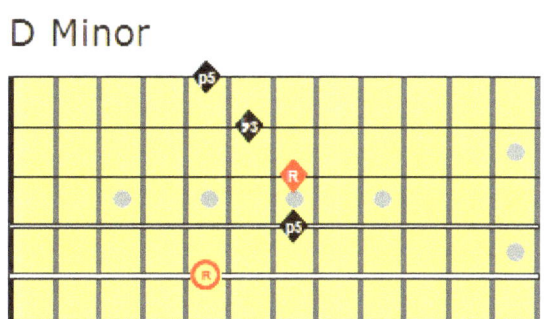

C Minor

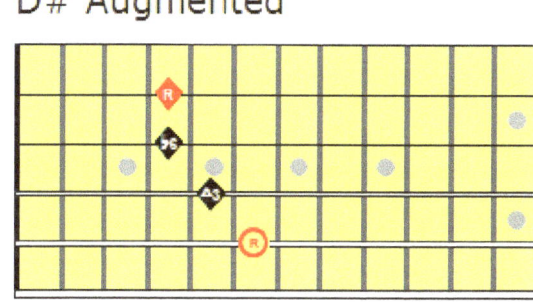

D Minor

D# Augmented

G HINDUSTAN SCALE LICKS

Here you can play a repetive lick and also play some octaves in bar four.

In this lick I'm playing a descending run on the high E and B strings.

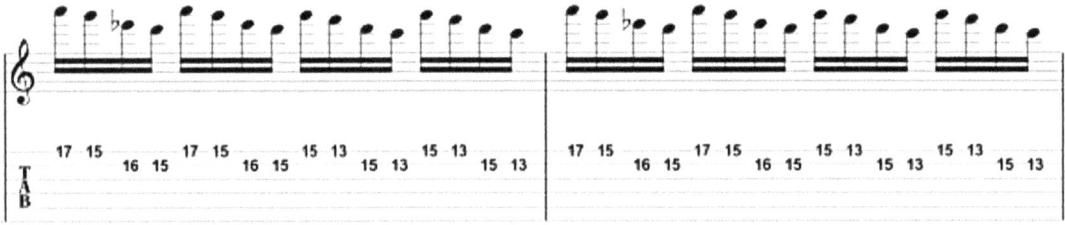

This lick uses some repetition and ends with vibrato.

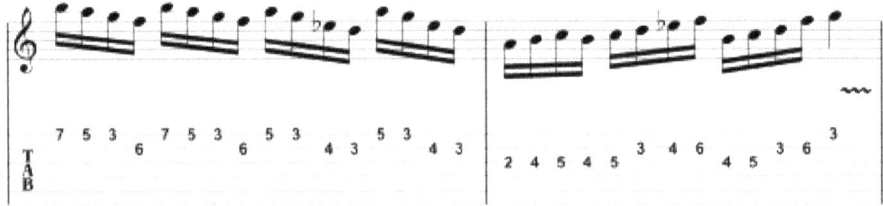

HUNGARIAN GYPSY PERSIAN SCALE

Intervals

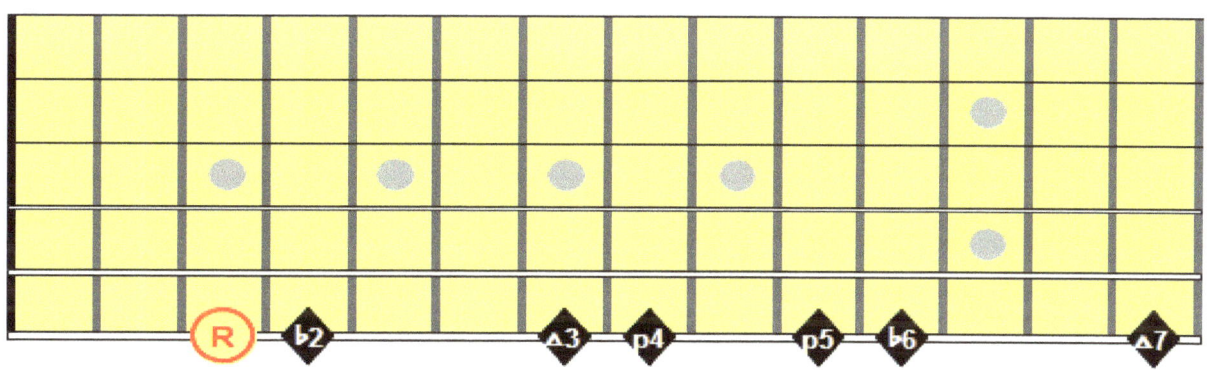

IN STEPS: H W + H H W H W + H

> Compared to the major scale, the Hungarian Gypsy
> Persian scale has a flat 2nd, and a flat 6th.

SOME HISTORY OF MUSIC IN HUNGARY AND PERSIA

In **Hungary**, Opera, Classical, Gypsy, Yiddish, and Roma music are popular. The genesis of conventional ethnic Hungarian gypsy music dates back to the independence war of the mid 1800s. This form of music was mainly to stimulate the emotions of the crowds and persuade them to join the army.

Franz Liszt is one such person who among his other works is best recognized for his Hungarian Rhapsodies, which were a blend of classical and Hungarian gypsy influences. He established the Budapest Music Academy, which became a beacon of musical influence in Hungary throughout the 19th and 20th centuries.

In Persia: From the Sassanian era (third to seventh century a.d.), they thrived on the initial native Persian sources involving music. These give names of musicians, their actions, and images of the instruments they played. The most famous Sassanian musician was Barbad, court musician to King Khosros II (591-628 A.D.). He became renowned for his genius, for the richness of his interpretations, and for some major numbers of musical compositions and systems.

SOME G HUNGARIAN GYPSY PERSIAN SCALE SHAPES

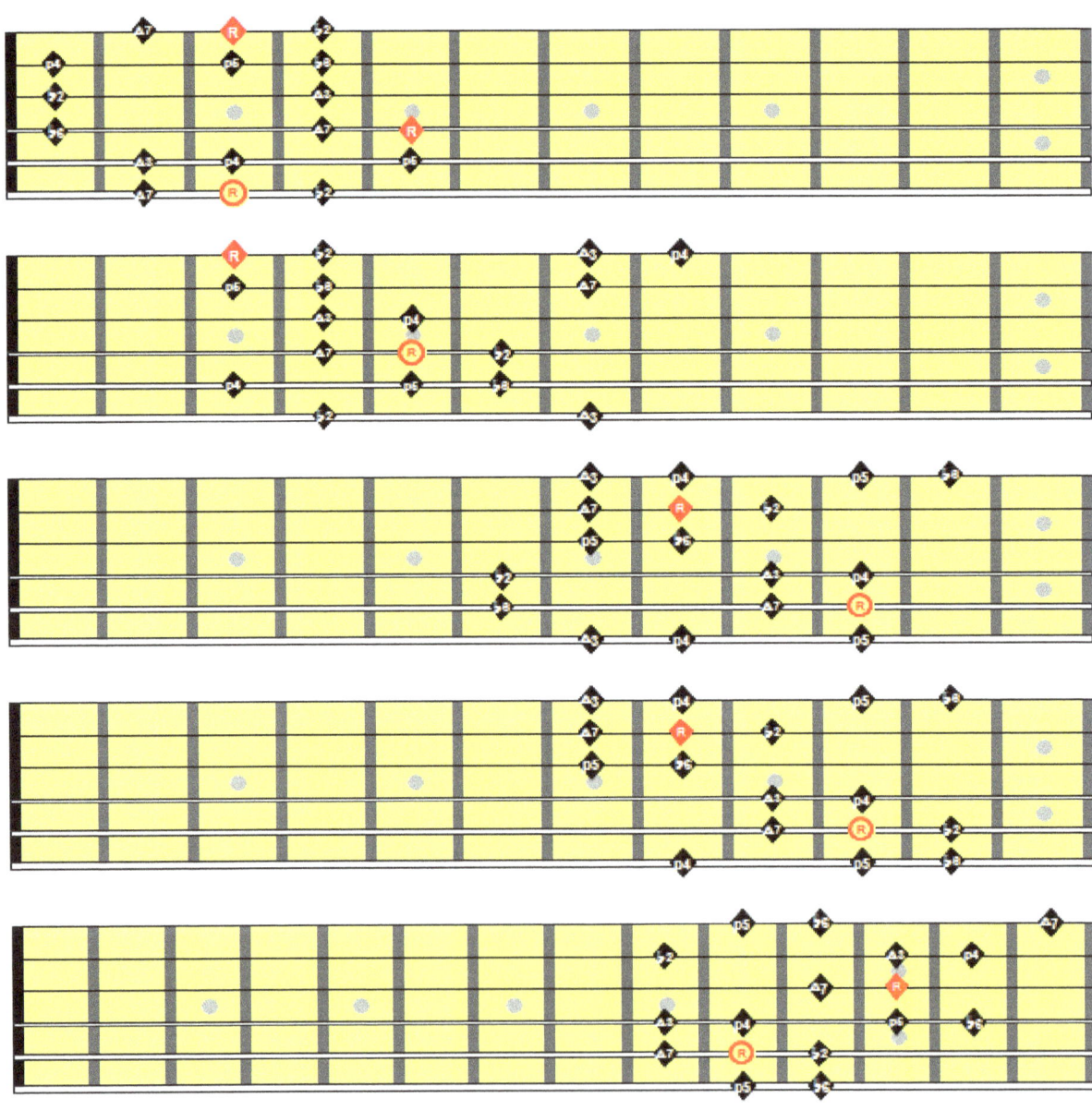

HUNGARIAN GYPSY PERSIAN SCALE

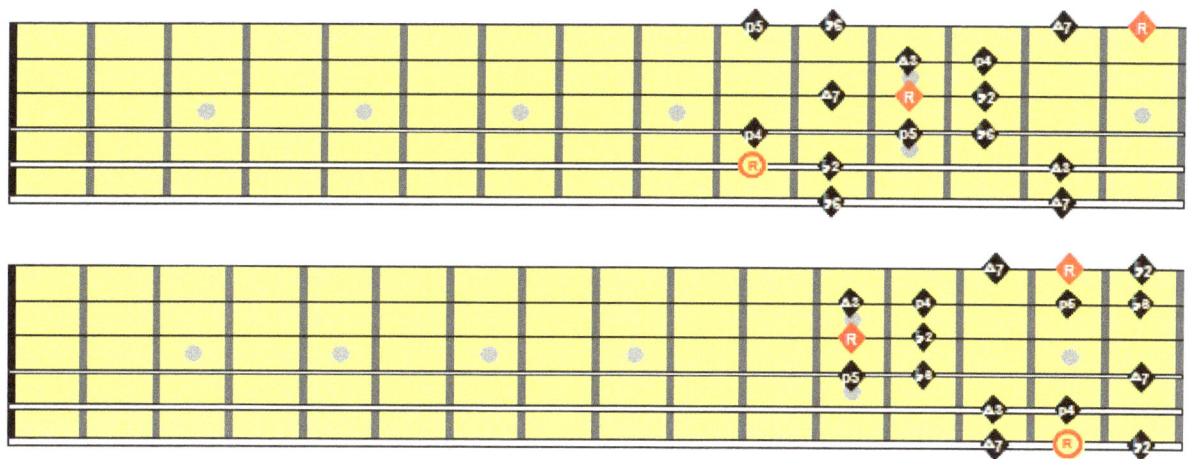

SOME CHORDS FORMED FROM THE G HUNGARIAN GYPSY PERSIAN SCALE

G Major

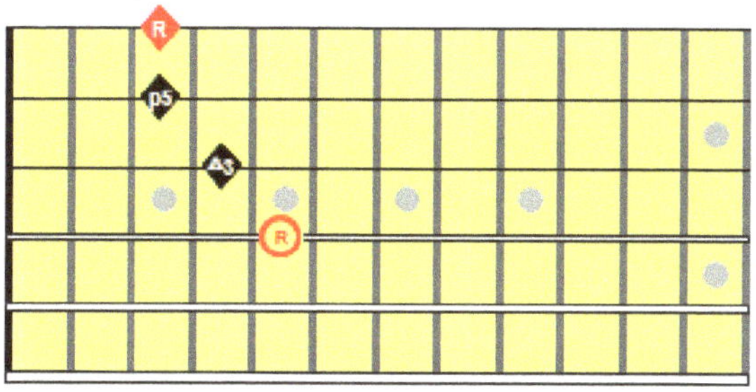

G# Major

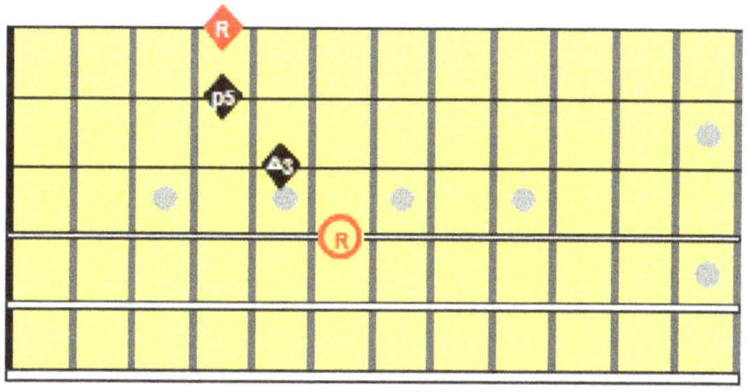

B Major

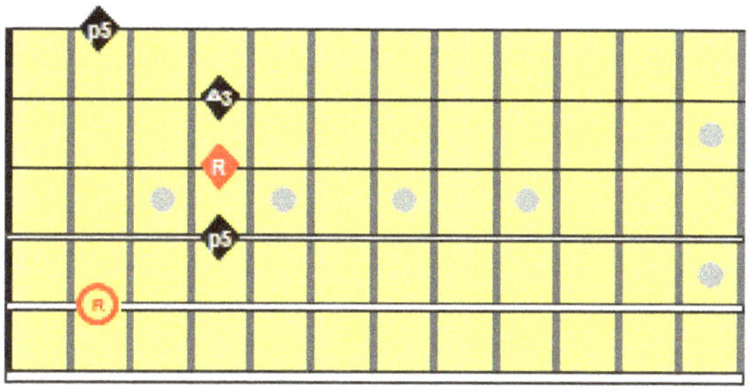

C Minor

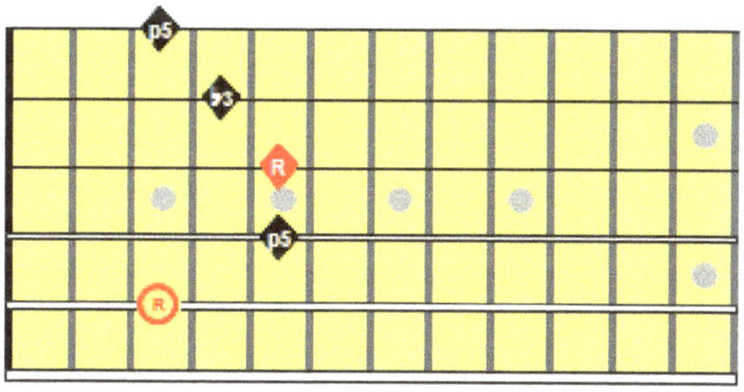

D 7b5

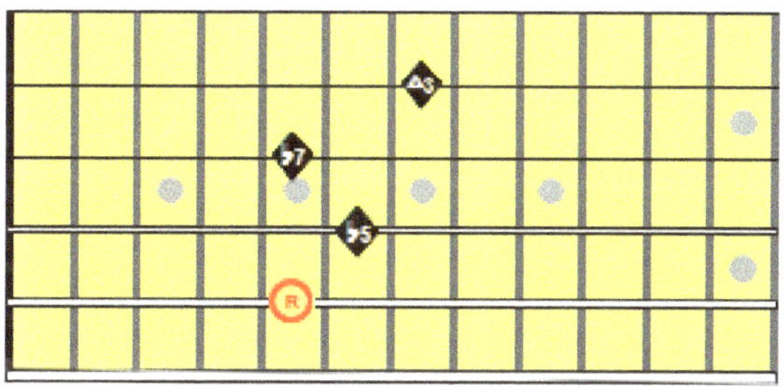

D# Augmented

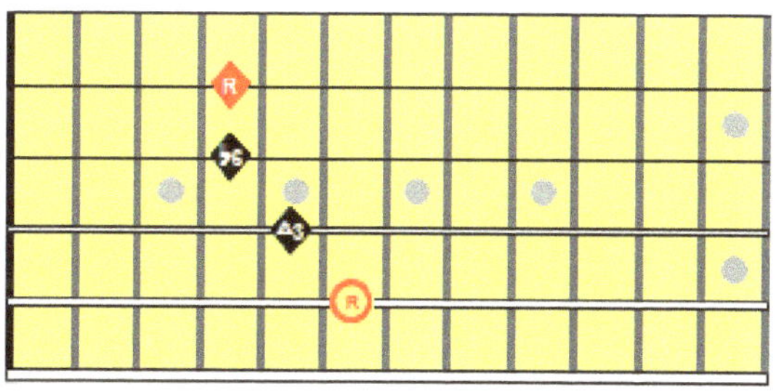

G HUNGARIAN GYPSY PERSIAN SCALE LICKS

This lick is played over a G augmented chord.

This lick is played over a Gsus4 chord.

The GYPSY JAZZ GUITAR

JAPANESE (ICHIKOSUCHO) SCALE

Intervals

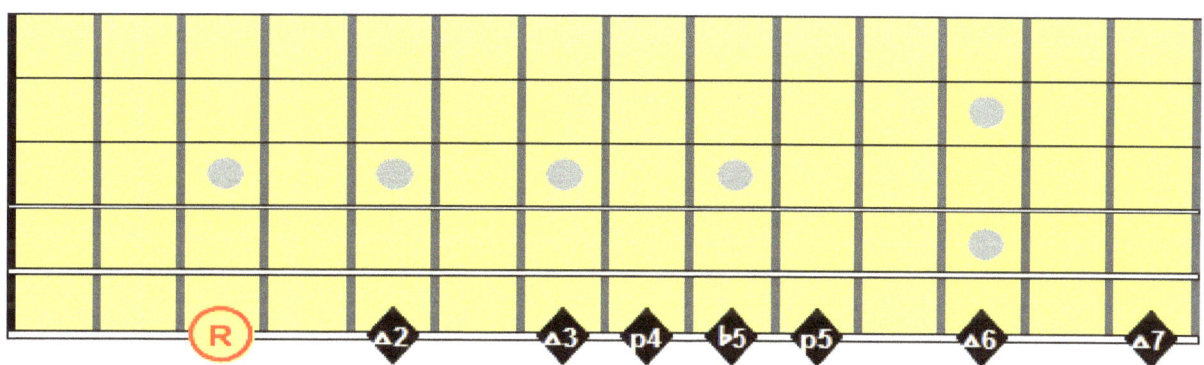

IN STEPS: W W H H H W W

Compared to the major scale, the Japanese (Ichikosucho) scale
has the same formula except for one extra note: A flat fifth.
The Japanese (Ichikosucho) scale is an eight-tone scale.

SOME HISTORY OF JAPANESE MUSIC

In the mid 1980s, when 'world music' became a commonly established phrase,
some Japanese started to look at themselves and speculate what their own
country had to offer. There was time-honored music, but this had frequently

been conserved and held little association to most Japanese people. Pop music conversely, had lost practically any hint of anything innately Japanese. Japanese musicians found themselves attracted to the music of Okinawa, even though to many Japanese, Okinawa can appear rather distant and even unfamiliar.

In Japan, there are many great guitarists such as: Takayoshi Ohmura, Masahiro Andoh, and Anchang. Electric guitar is popular especially among young Japanese people.

SOME G JAPANESE (ICHIKOSUCHO) SCALE SHAPES

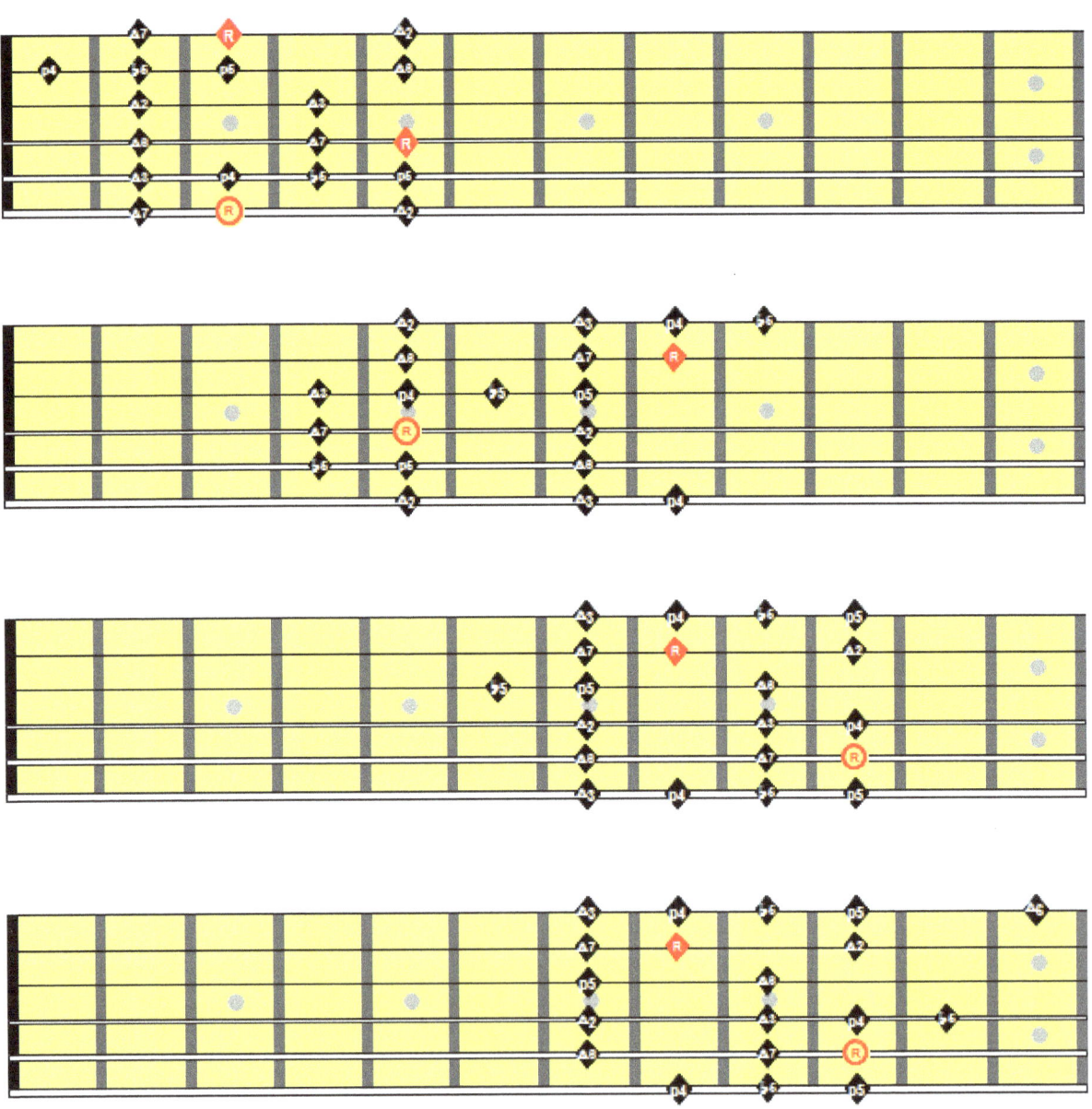

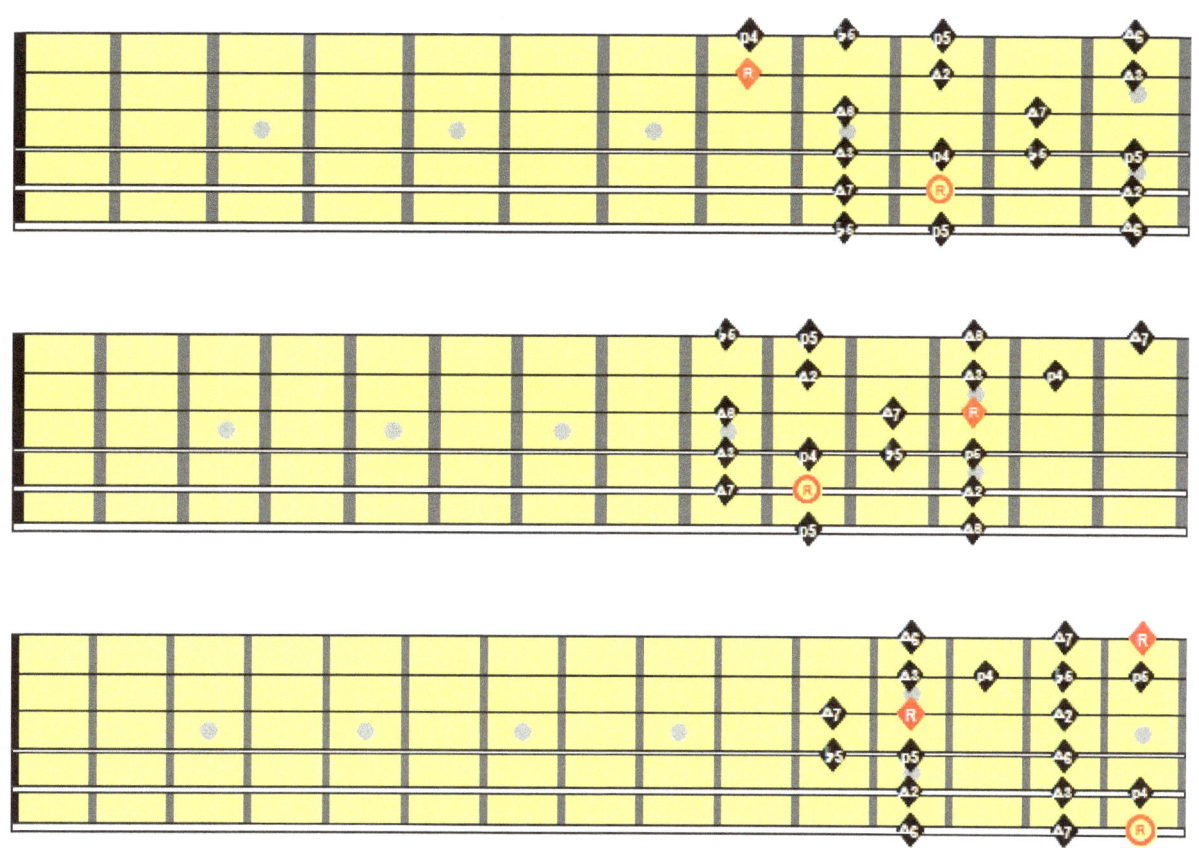

SOME CHORDS FORMED FROM THE G JAPANESE (ICHIKOSUCHO) SCALE

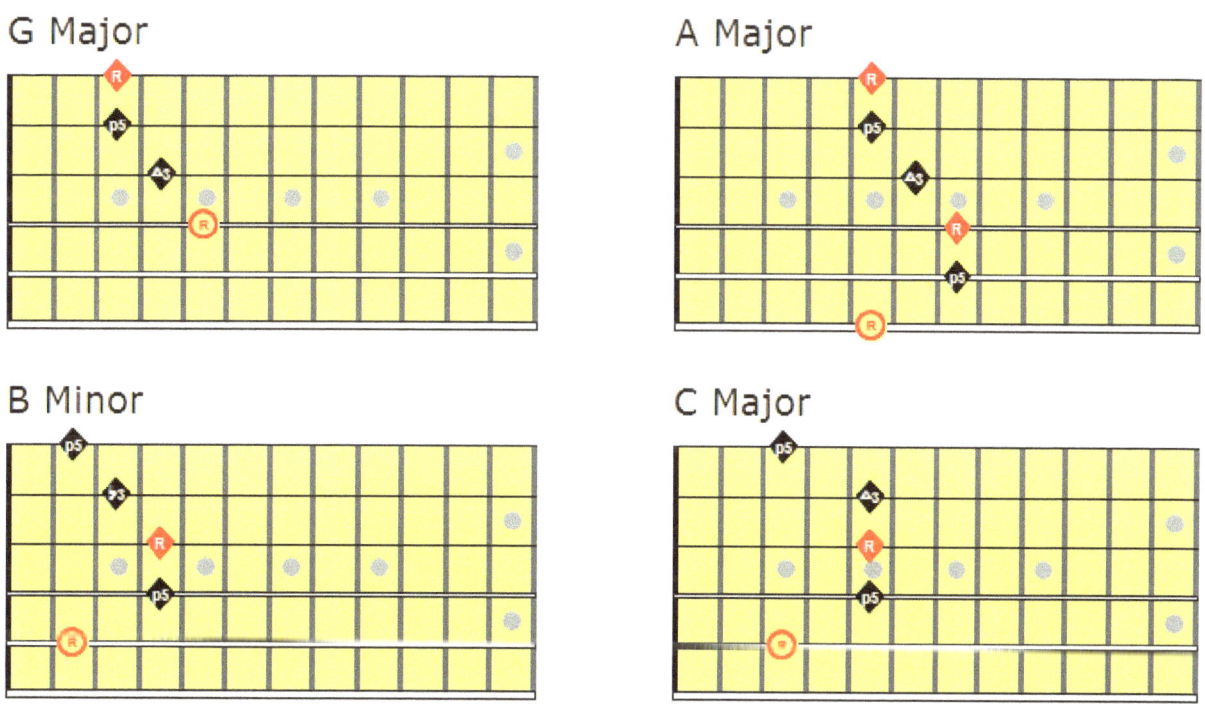

G Major

A Major

B Minor

C Major

C# Diminished

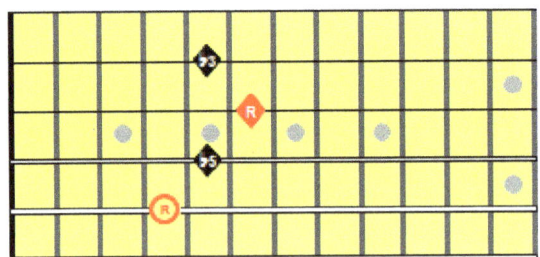

D Major

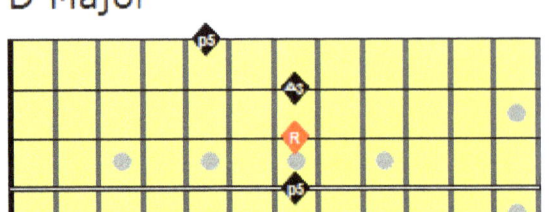

G JAPANESE (ICHIKOSUCHO) SCALE LICKS

This lick uses some interesting 16th note triplets, arrpegiation, and some melodic repetitive licks.

This lick is played over a GMaj7 chord.

JAVANESE SCALE

Intervals

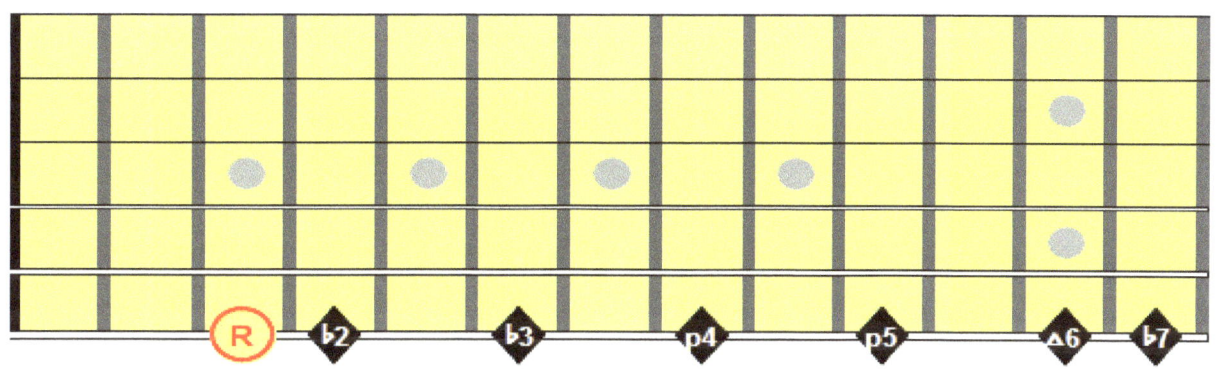

IN STEPS: H W W W W H

Compared to the major scale, the Javanese
scale has a flat 2nd, flat 3rd, and a flat 7th.

JAVANESE STRINGED INSTRUMENTS

The **Celempung** is a large archaic zither rarely used in the modern Javanese
gamelan.

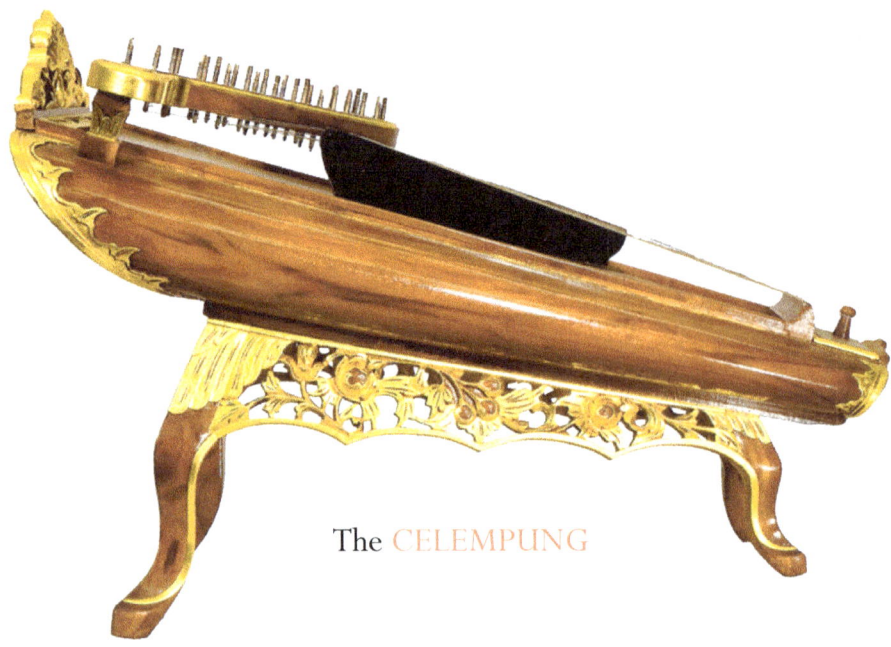

The CELEMPUNG

The **Kacapi** is another form of zither usually combined with suling.

The KACAPI

SOME HISTORY OF JAVANESE 'GAMELAN' MUSIC

Gamelan is a drumming-dominated musical group. It is also recognized as a Gong-chime musical ensemble. This musical band consists of bronze gongs and metallophones. Besides Indonesia, gamelan is played in Malaysia too.

Gamelan music is in polyphonic stratification composition. It means the music is composed by layers of straightforward melody lines or rhythm patterns. There are five categories in this polyphonic stratification:

1. Nuclear Theme
2. Elaboration
3. Punctuation
4. Counter-Melody
5. Rhythm

SOME G JAVANESE SCALE SHAPES

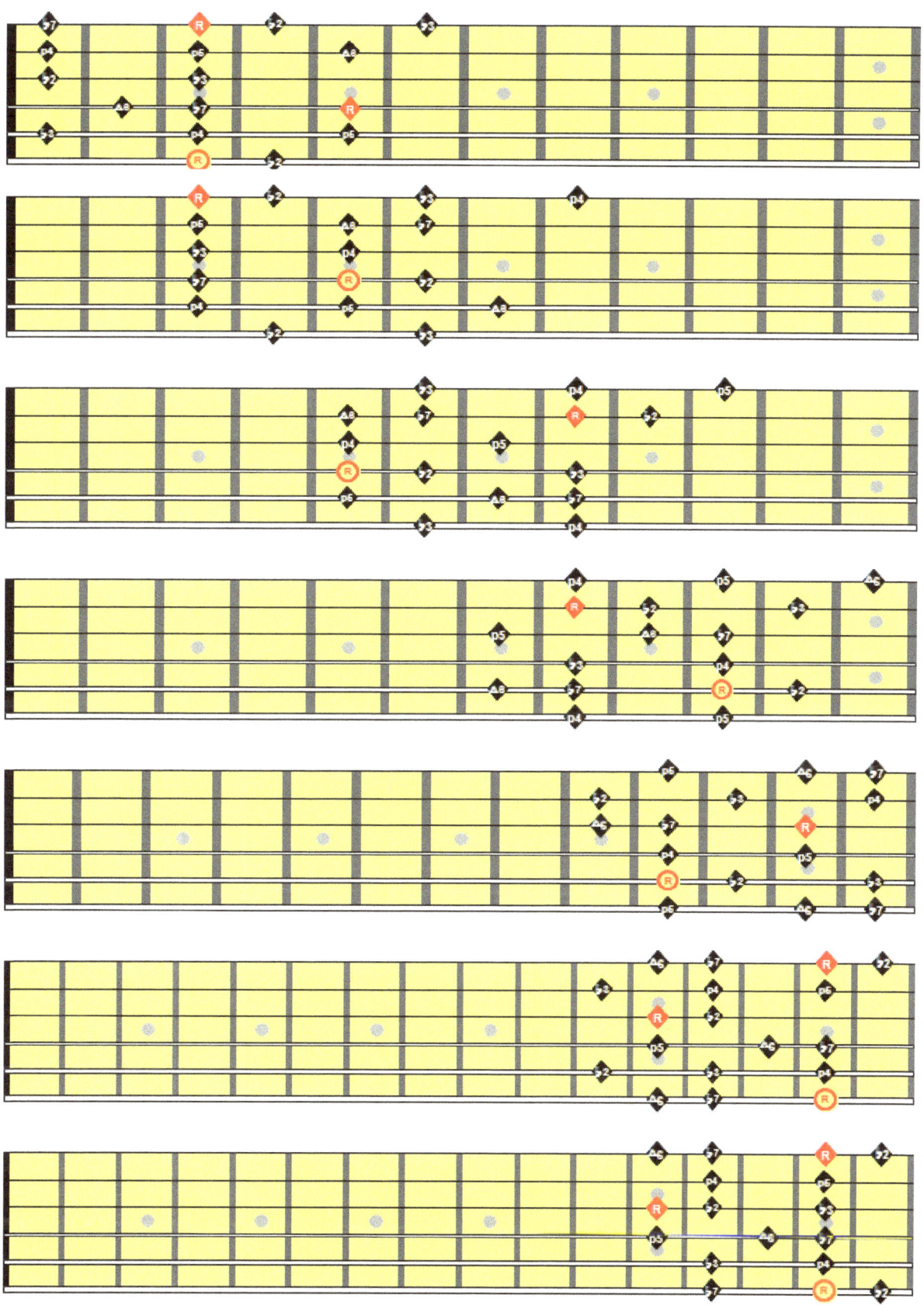

SOME CHORDS FORMED FROM THE G JAVANESE SCALE

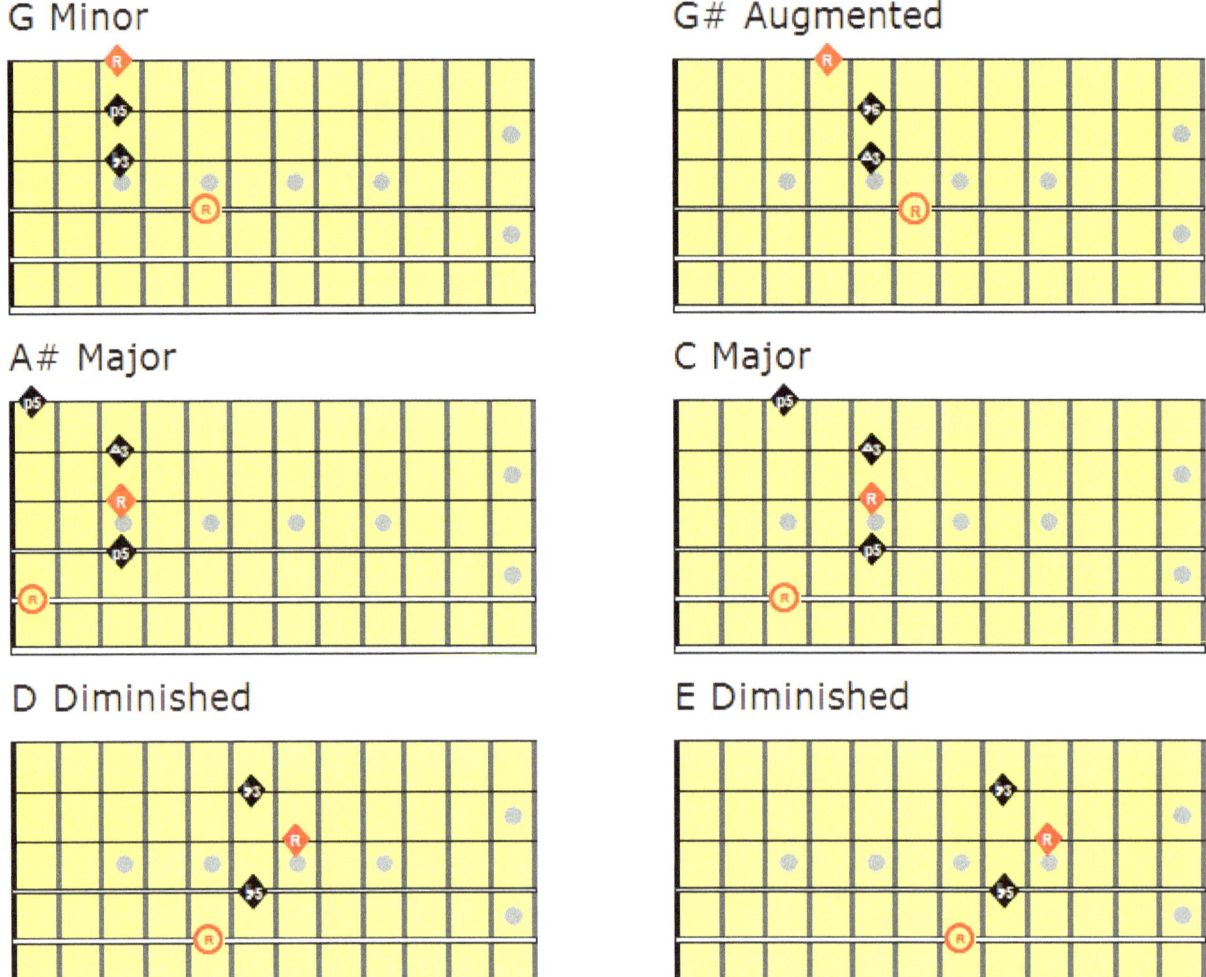

G Minor

G# Augmented

A# Major

C Major

D Diminished

E Diminished

G JAVANESE SCALE LICKS

Rock out on some 16th notes, some 16th note triplets and some 32nd notes in this lick.

Play this lick over a G minor chord.

This lick is played over a G minor arpeggio

JEWISH (ADONIA MALAKH) SCALE

Intervals

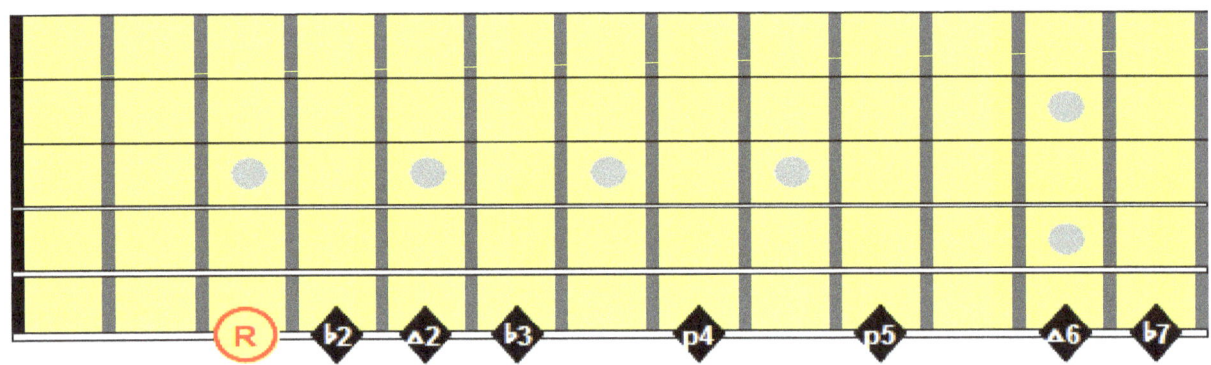

IN STEPS: H H H W W W H

Compared to the major scale, the Jewish (Adonia Malakh) scale has a flat 2nd, flat 3rd, and a flat 7th. The Jewish (Adonia Malakh) is an eight-tone scale.

JEWISH STRINGED INSTRUMENTS

A Kinnōr comes from the root "to twang." **Nebel** means "a skin bottle," perhaps referring to the shape of the sound box. Most authorities say **kinnōr** is a lyre and **nebel** is a harp. However, there is some confusion between these terms. Some feel that the main difference between them might be that of size and number of strings.

The KINNŌR

The *nebel* was often played with the kinnōr (1 Kings 10:12) or with other instruments (Isaiah 5:12). It was used in the temple (2 Chronicles 5:12).

The NEBEL

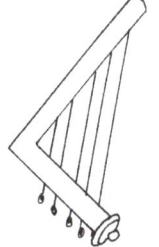

SOME HISTORY OF JEWISH MUSIC

Music was always a part of the community, but it took on new meaning with the assembly of the Temple at Jerusalem. From the instant that King David "danced with all his strength," in front of the Holy Ark as it entered Jerusalem; all sacred ceremonies would be accompanied by music. In the place of worship itself, there was a singing group with some instrumental accompaniment that sang as the daily and unique occasion sacrifices were brought. The First Temple period, from the 9th century B.C.E. to the year 586 B.C.E. was the time when the Psalms were composed. Their community performances were most likely Temple based. By the time of the second Temple, in the next five centuries, the order of which Psalms would be chanted at which service became resolutely recognized. The tradition of reciting the daily Psalm practiced in synagogues today is a continuation of that tradition.

The first mention of musical instruments in the Bible is to be found in the Book of Genesis. These two instruments, the harp (Hebrew: nevel) and the lyre (Hebrew: kinnor), are the two stringed instruments most commonly mentioned in the Bible.

SOME G JEWISH (ADONAI MALAKH) SCALE SHAPES

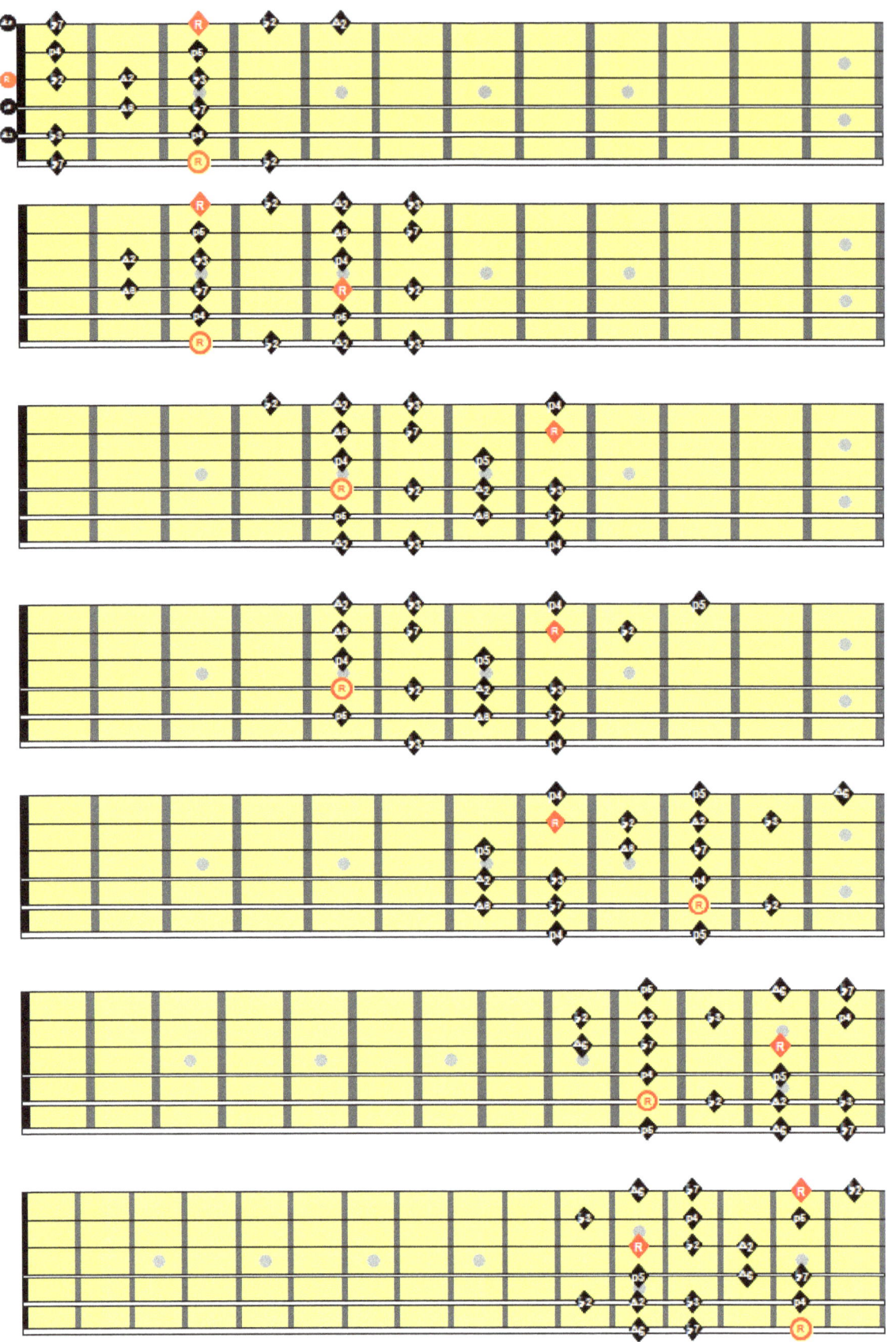

SOME CHORDS FORMED FROM THE G JEWISH (ADONI MALAKH) SCALE

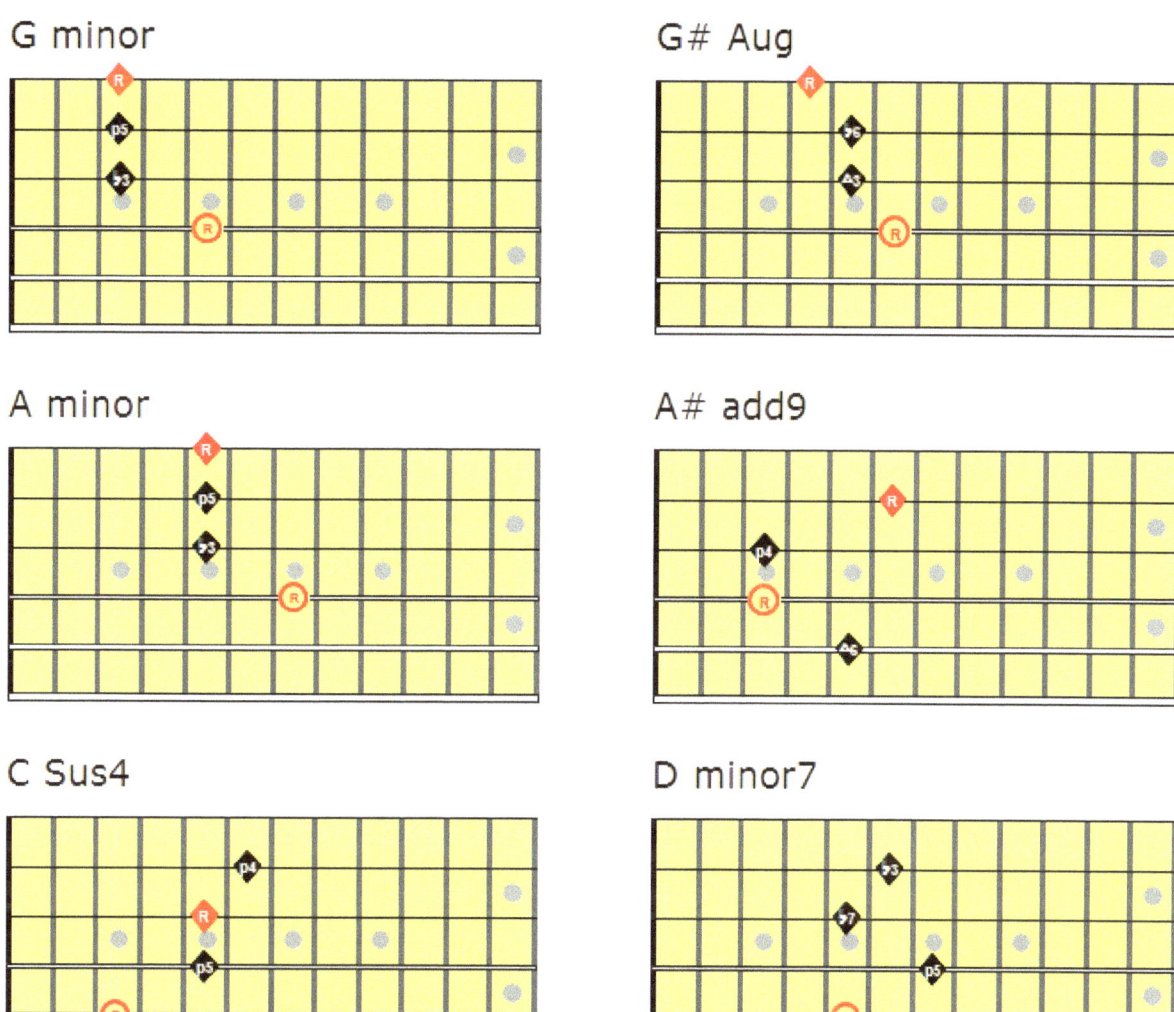

G minor

G# Aug

A minor

A# add9

C Sus4

D minor7

G JEWISH (ADONIA MALAKH) SCALE LICKS

Start this lick out by descending and spanning the neck guitar using a sequence pattern that utilizes the high E, B, and G strings. Then go into an ascending lick.

In this lick play the octaves.

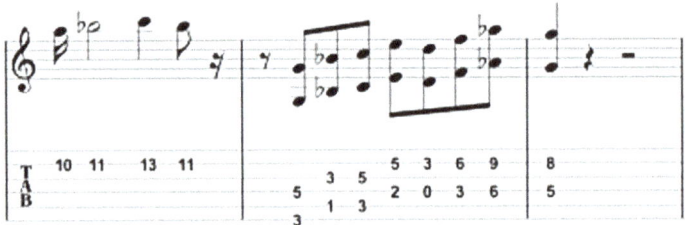

Famous Jewish Guitar Player
YOSSI PIAMENTA

MOORISH PHRYGIAN SCALE

Intervals

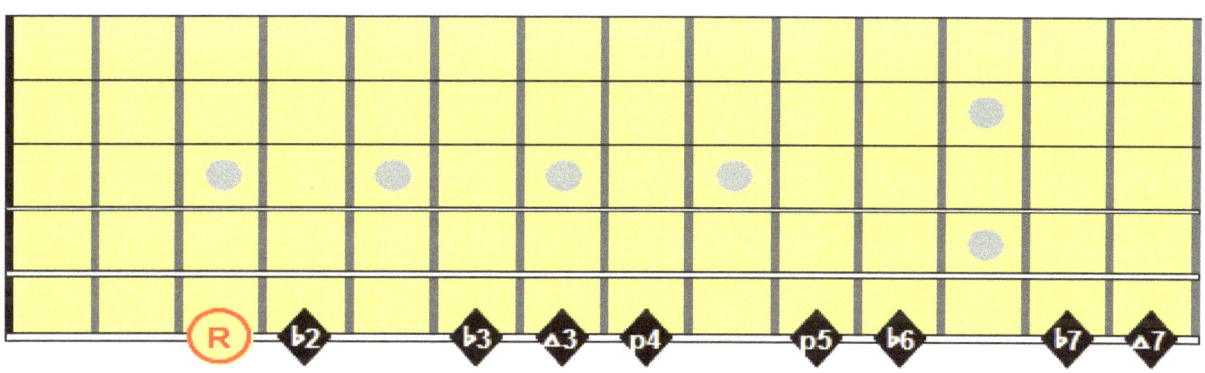

IN STEPS: H W H H W H W H

> Compared to the major scale, the Moorish Phrygian
> scale has a flat 2nd, flat 3rd, flat 6th, and a flat 7th.
> he Moorish Phrygian scale is a 9-tone scale.

SOME HISTORY OF MOORISH MUSIC

Andalusian classical music is a style of Moorish music established across North Africa in Morocco, Algeria, Tunisia, and Libya. It originates out of the music of Al-Andalus (Muslim Iberia) between the 9th and 15th centuries. Andalusian classical music was supposedly born in the Emirate of Cordoba

(Al-Andalus) in the 9th century. The Persian musician, residing in Iraq, Ziryâb (d. 857), who later became court musician of Abd al-Rahman II in Cordoba, is occasionally recognized with its invention. Later, the poet, musician, and philosopher Ibn Bajjah (d. 1139) of Saragossa is said to have combined the method of Ziryâb with Western approaches to create a completely new approach that stretched across Iberia and North Africa.

Many of the musical instruments that are now used in Western music were initially brought to Europe during this Moorish occupation of Spain. These include the guitar, the lute, the violin the flute, various reed instruments, wind instruments, the harp, zither and many percussion instruments. Over the centuries in Europe the Moorish versions of these instruments steadily evolved in to the form we are familiar with today.

SOME G MOORISH PHYRGIAN SCALE SHAPES

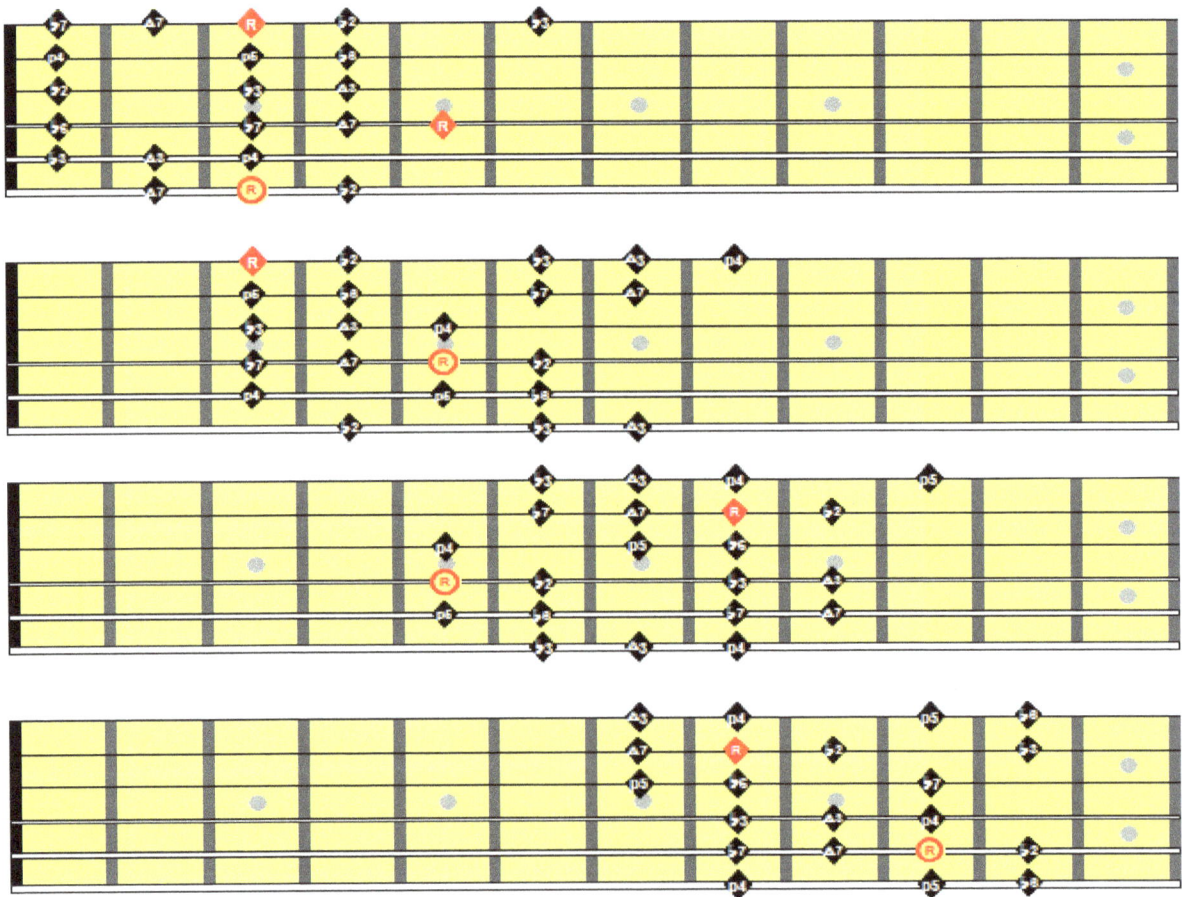

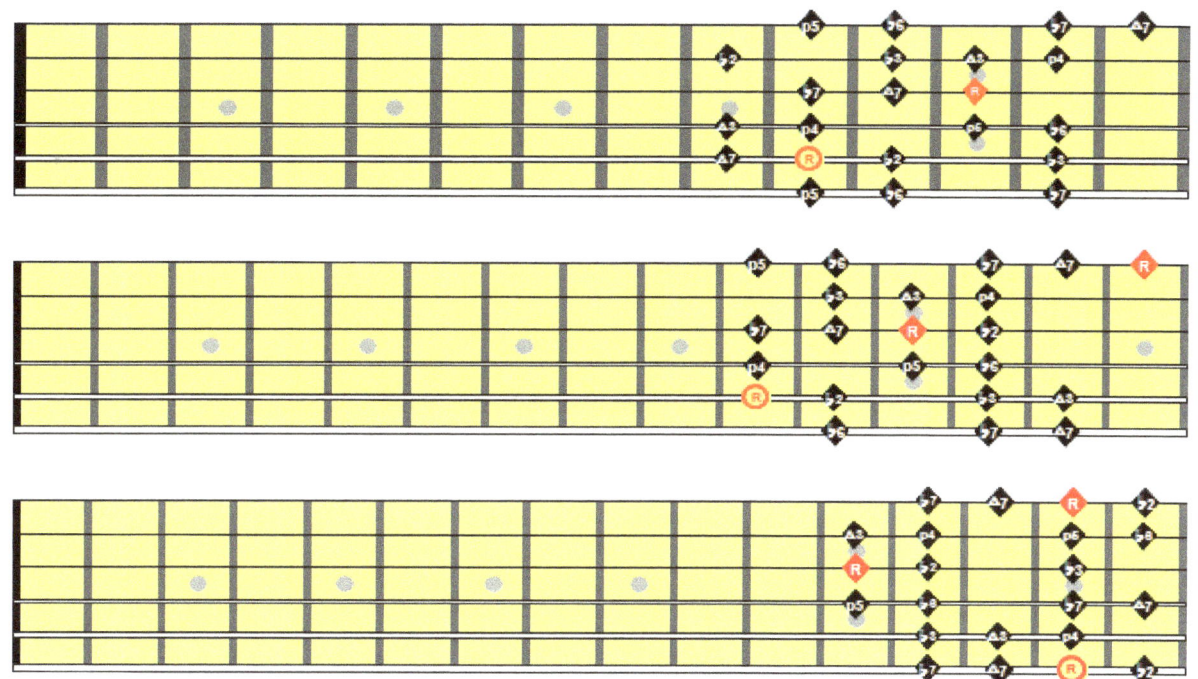

SOME CHORDS FORMED FROM THE G MOORISH PHRYGIAN SCALE

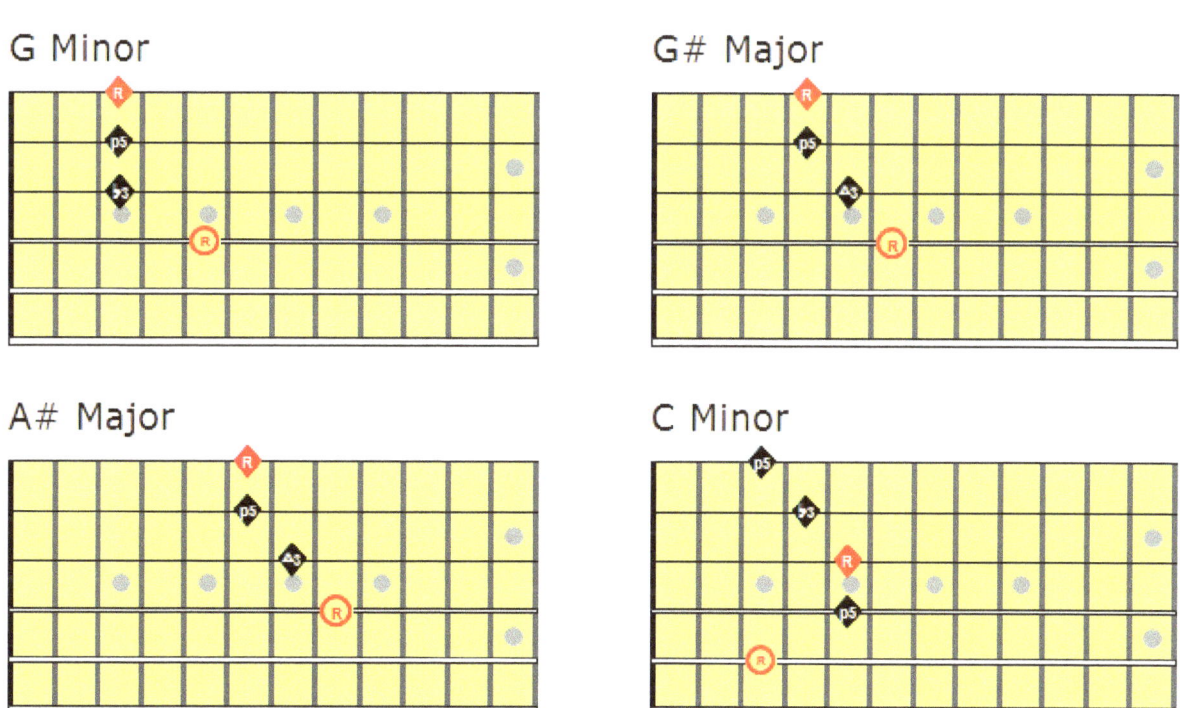

D Diminished

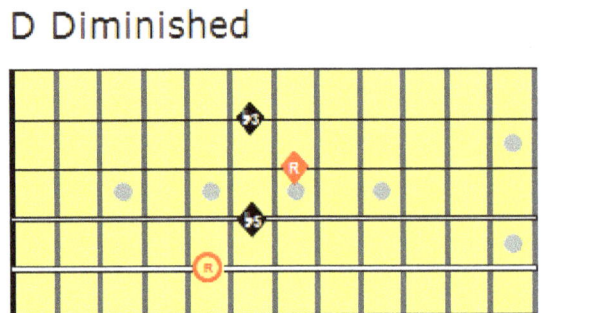

D# Major

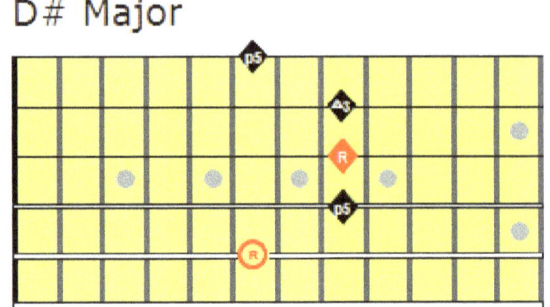

G MOORISH PHRYGIAN SCALE LICKS

This is a speed metal lick in the style of Yngwie Malmsteen. Don't worry if you can't play it super duper fast.

You can jam out over a Gsus4 chord in this lick.

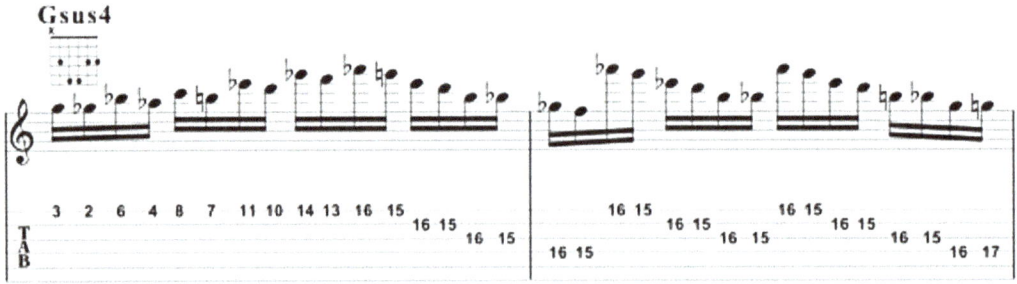

G PROMETHEUS NEAPOLITAN SCALE

Intervals

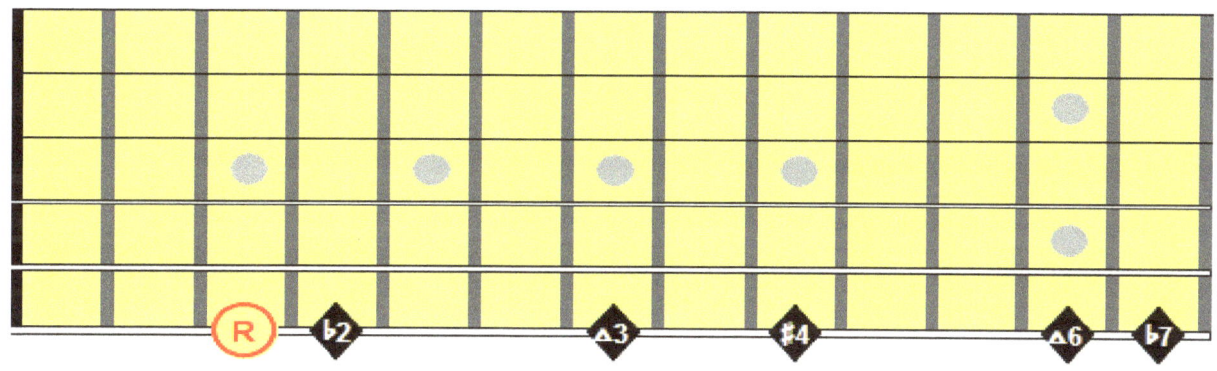

IN STEPS: H W + H W W + H H

> Compared to the major scale, the Prometheus Neapolitan scale has a flat 2nd, sharp 4th, NO 5th, and a flat 7th.
> The Prometheus Neapolitan scale is a 6-tone scale.

SOME HISTORY OF THE PROMETHEUS NEAPOLITAN SCALE

The Prometheus Neapolitan scale can be really useful if you are looking forward to create cheerful music as it belongs to the group of Major scales. It is mainly used in ethnic music or modal jazz improvisation.

SOME G PROMETHEUS NEAPOLITAN SCALE SHAPES

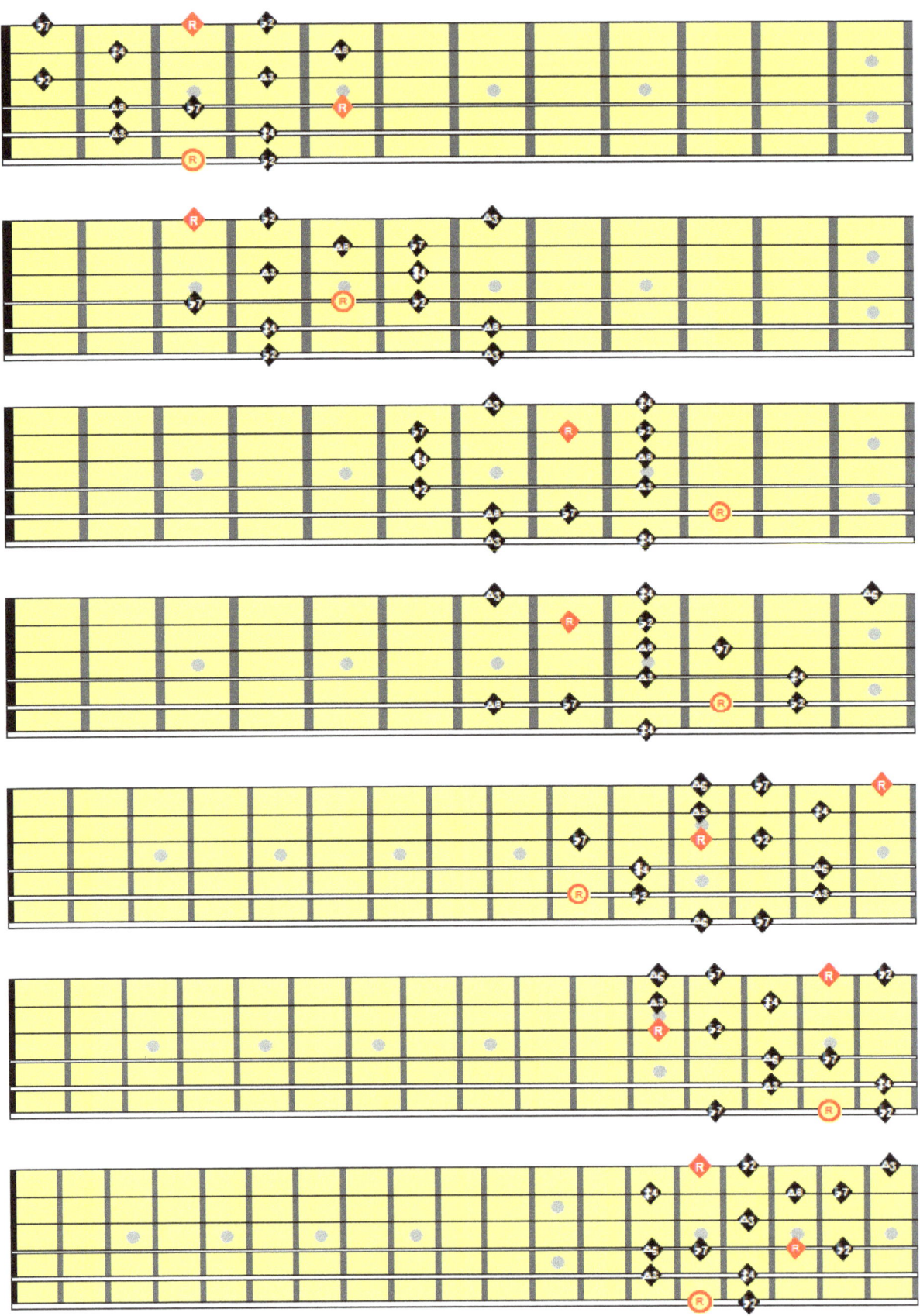

SOME CHORDS FORMED FROM THE
G PROMETHEUS NEAPOLITAN SCALE

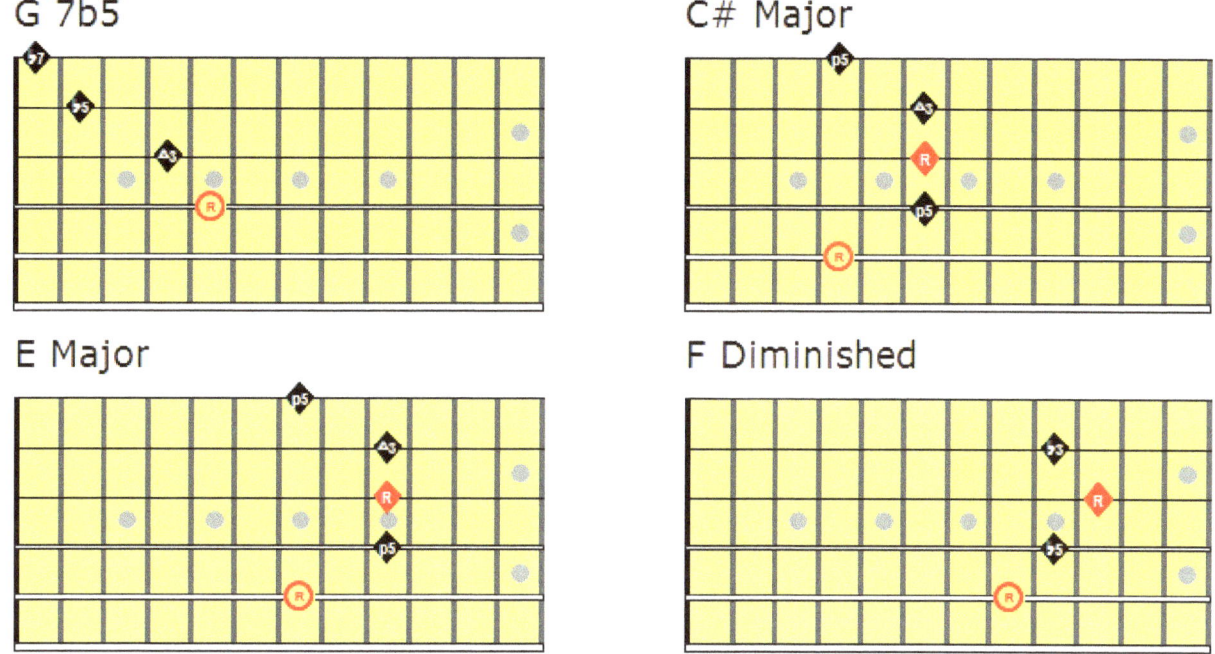

G 7b5

C# Major

E Major

F Diminished

G PROMETHEUS NEAPOLITAN SCALE LICKS

In this lick you can play some 1/16 note triplets.

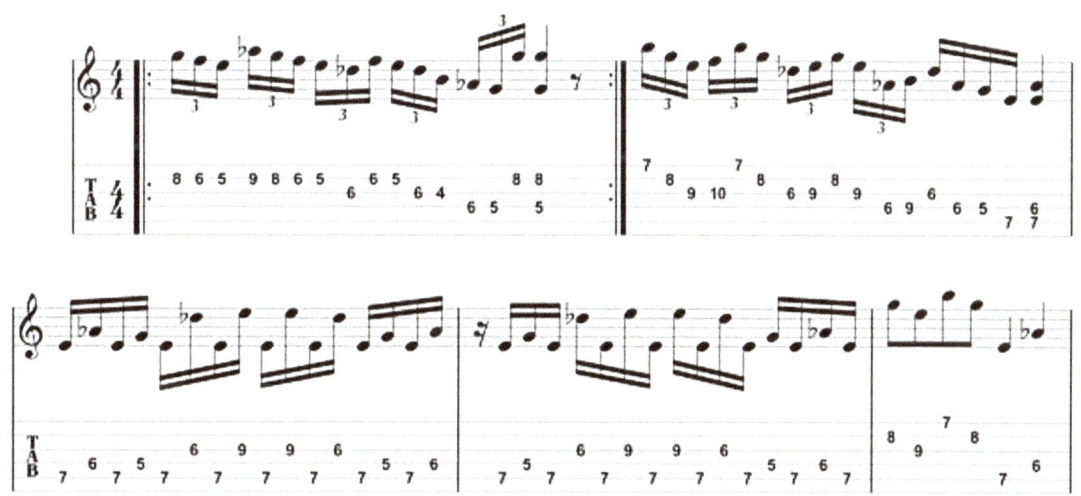

In this lick you can use 1/16 notes and 1/16 note triplets.

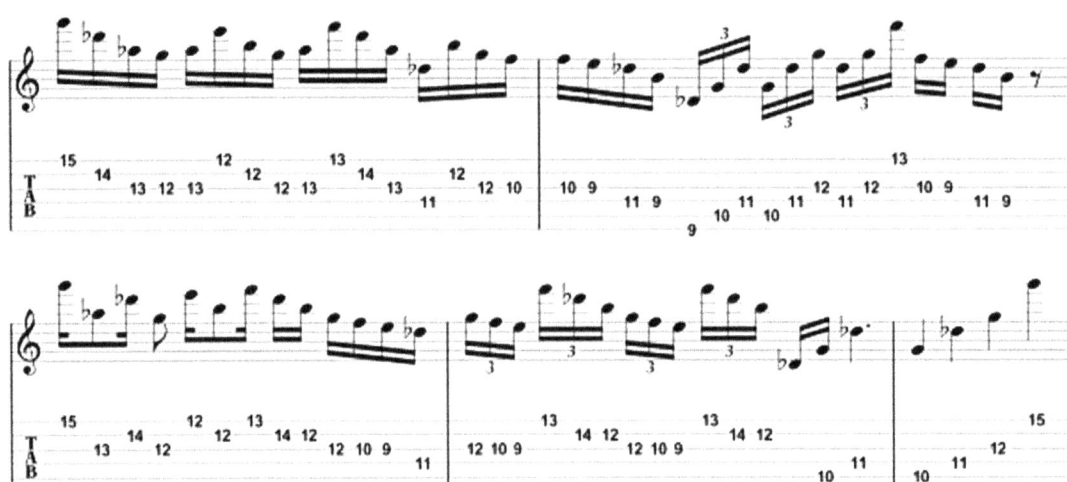

This is a pedal lick

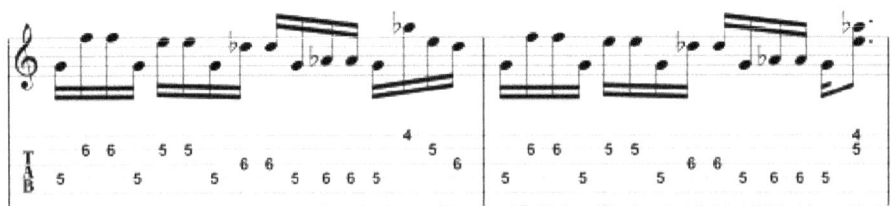

ROMANIAN MINOR SCALE

Intervals

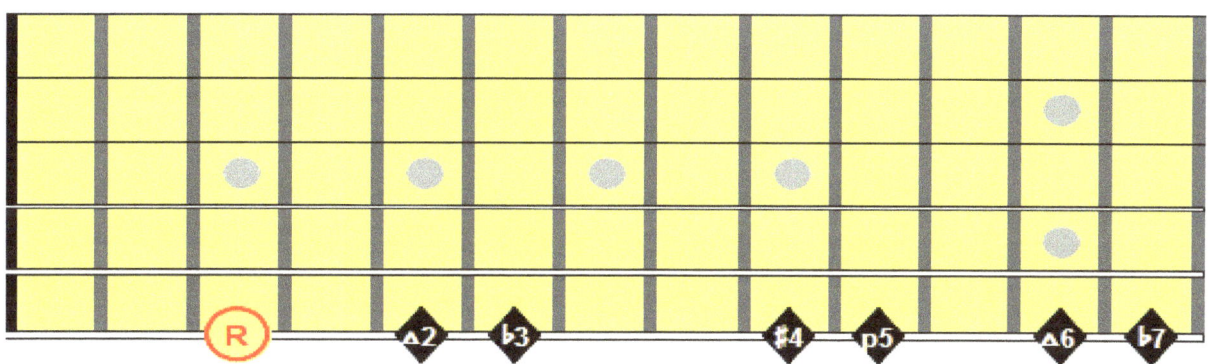

IN STEPS: W H W + H H W H

Compared to the major scale, the Romanian minor scale
has a flat 3rd, sharp 4th, and a flat 7th.

SOME HISTORY OF ROMANIAN MUSIC

The initial music was played on a range of pipes with rhythmical accompaniment later added by a cobza. A cobza is a Romanian lute-like instrument. This approach can still be found in Moldavian Carpathian regions of Vrancea and Bucovina and with the Hungarian Csango minority.

The bagpipe was admired from medieval times, as it was in most European countries, but became uncommon in current times before a 20th century renewal. Since its beginning, the violin has influenced the music in all regions by becoming the main melody instrument. Each region has its own mixture of instruments, old and new, and its own exceptional sound. This continues to expand to the present day with the most current add-ons being electric keyboards and drum sets.

SOME G ROMANIAN MINOR SCALE SHAPES

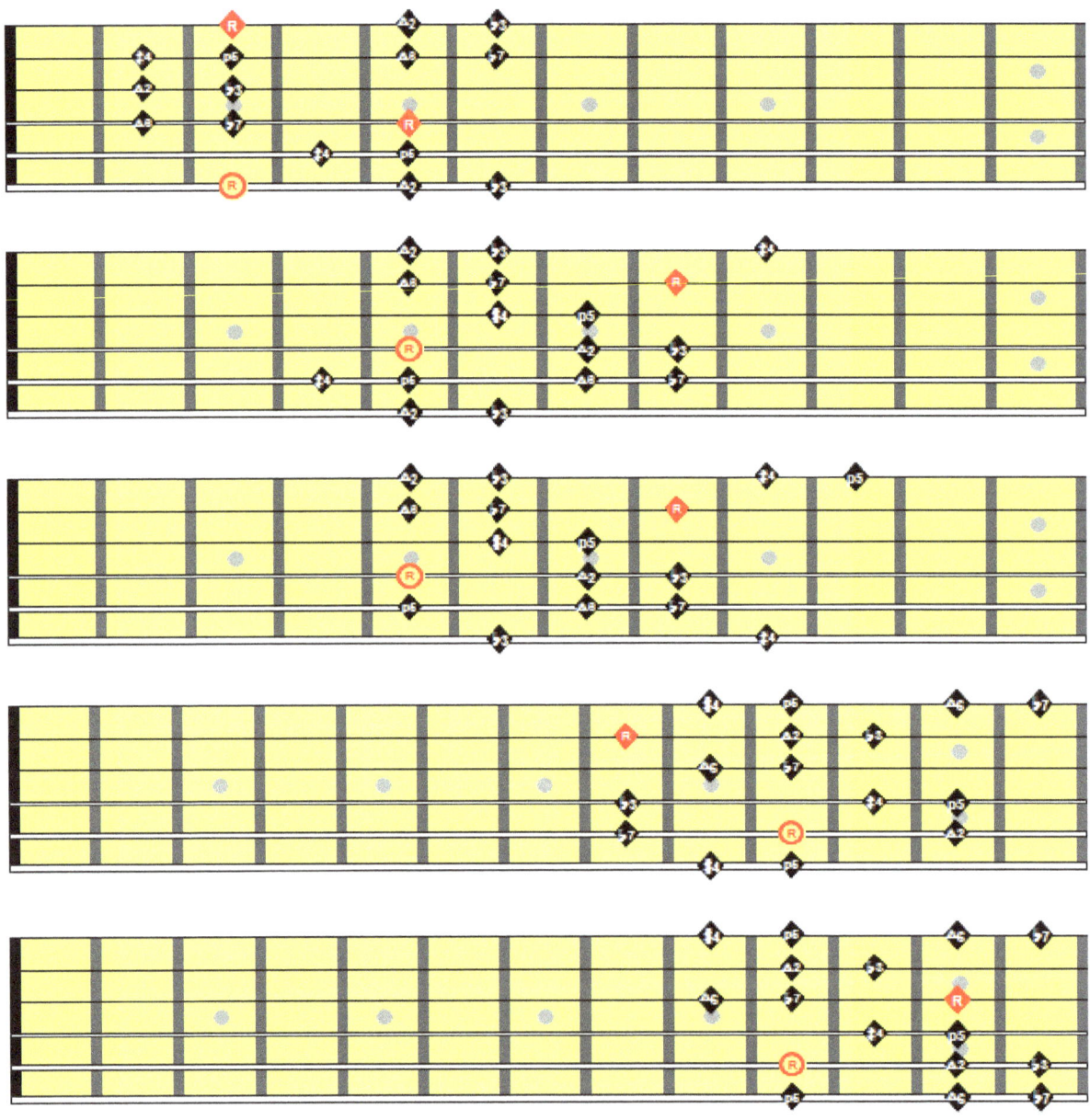

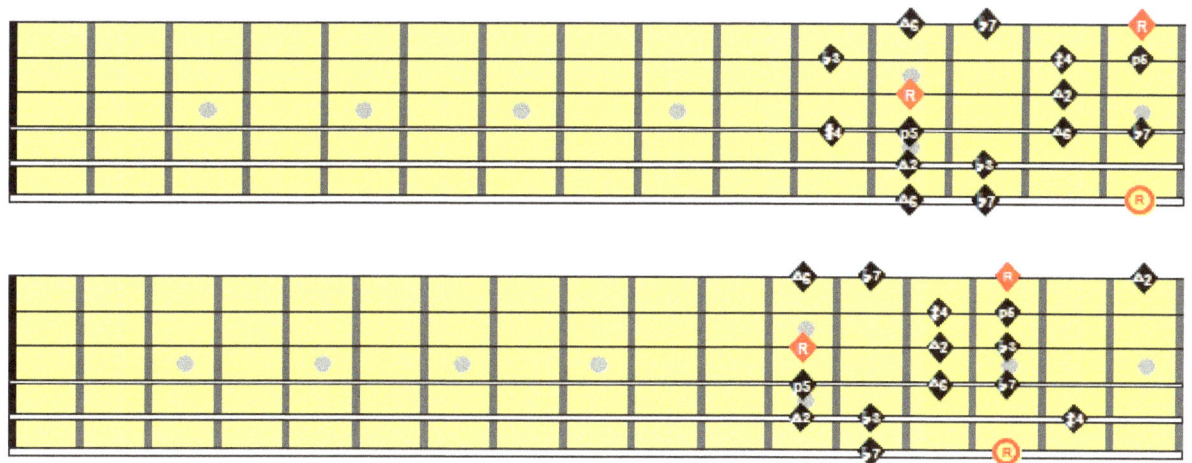

SOME CHORDS FORMED FROM THE G ROMANIAN MINOR SCALE

G Minor

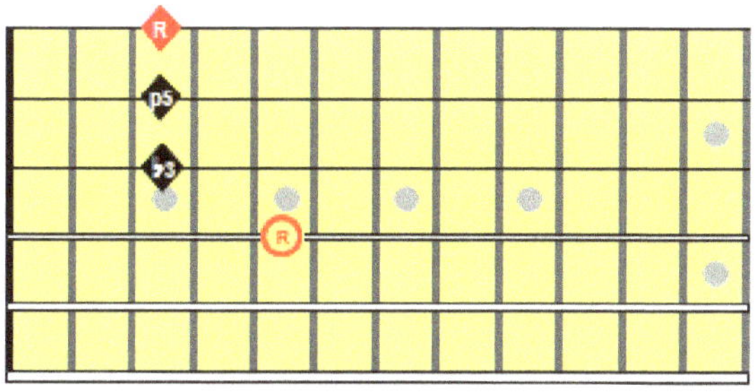

A Major

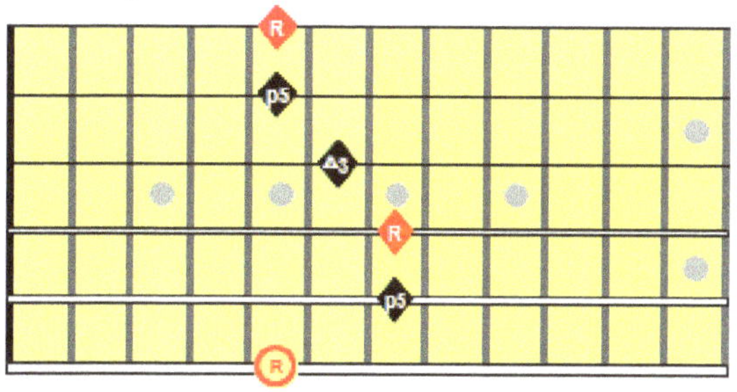

A# Major

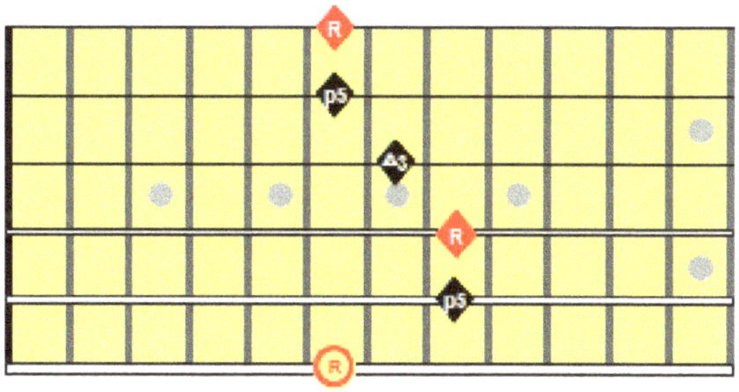

C# Diminished

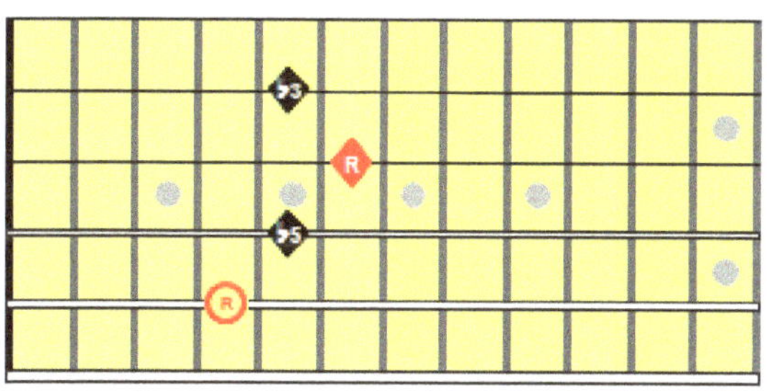

D Minor

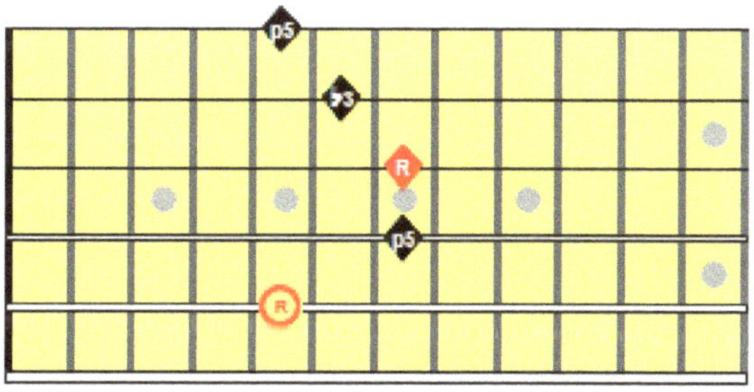

E Diminished

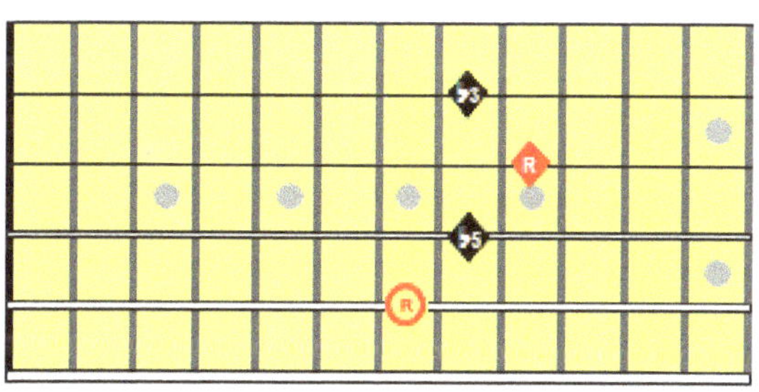

G ROMANIAN MINOR SCALE LICKS

In this lick I'm using a repetitive sequence and some 16th note triplets.

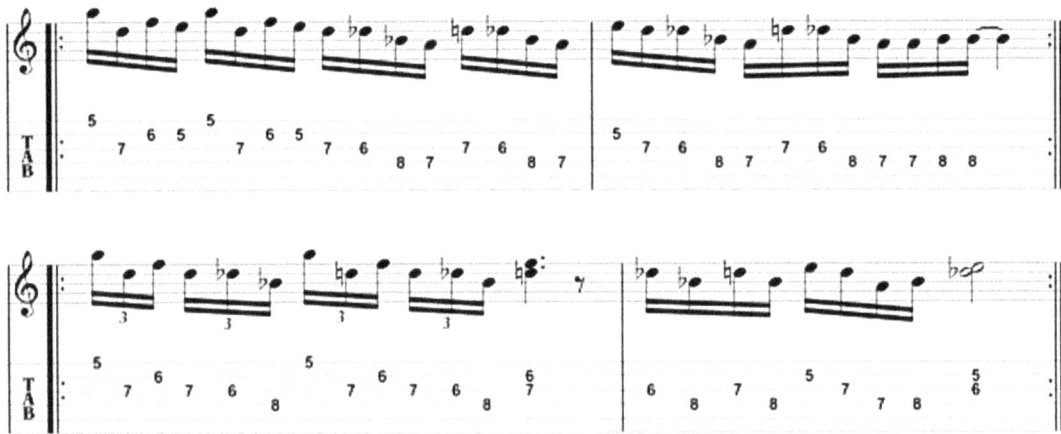

FURTHER READING

BOOKS

Belkadi, J.M. *Exotic Scales & Licks for Guitar*. Milwaukee: Hal Leonard Corporation, 2005.

Berle, Arnie. *Jazz & Popular Guitar*. New York: Amsco Publications, 1986.

Charupakorn, Joe. *Scales*, New York: Cherry Lane Music Company, 1999.

Eschete, Ron. *The Jazz Guitar Soloist*, California: Alfred Publishing Company, 1989.

Fisher, Jody. *Beginning Jazz Guitar: The Complete Jazz Guitar Method*, California: Alfred Publishing Company, 1995.

Fisher, Jody. *Intermediate Jazz Guitar: The Complete Jazz Guitar Method*, California: Alfred Publishing Company, 2006.

Fisher, Jody. *Mastering Chord/Melody: The Complete Jazz Guitar Method*, California: Alfred Publishing Company, 2006.

Fisher, Jody. *Mastering Improvisation: The Complete Jazz Guitar Method*, California: Alfred Publishing Company, 1995.

Gambale, Frank. *Improvisation Made Easier: An Improvisation Course for Intermediate to Advanced Guitarists*, California: Alfred Publishing Company, 1997.

Goodrick, Mick. *The Advancing Guitarist: Applying Guitar Concepts & Techniques*, Milwaukee: Hal Leonard Corporation, 1987.

Greene, Ted. *Chord Chemistry*, California: Alfred Publishing Company, 1971.

Johnson, Chad. *Guitarist's Guide To Scales Over Chords: The Foundation of Melodic Soloing*, Milwaukee: Hal Leonard Corporation, 2010.

Kolb, Tom. *Music Theory: Everything You Ever Wanted to Know But Were Afraid to Ask*, Milwaukee: Hal Leonard Corporation, 2005.

Kolb, Tom. *Modes for Guitar: A Complete Approach To Soloing*, Milwaukee: Hal Leonard Corporation, 2001.

Noad, F.M. *Solo Guitar Playing: A complete course of instruction in the techniques of guitar performance*, New York: Amsco Publications, 2009.

Satriani, Joe. *Guitar Secrets*, New York: Cherry Lane Music Company, 1993.

Stark, David. *Essential Skills For Sight-Reading Guitar: Kick-Start Your Reading Skills Now!*, California: Alfred Publishing Company, 1999.

WEB SITES

www.AndrewWasson.com

www.chordbook.com

www.chordie.com

http://classic.musictheory.net/81

www.classtab.org

www.freeguitarvideos.com

www.guitar.about.com/od/guitarlessons/u/lessons.htm

http://www.guitarlessons.com/jam-tracks/

www.GuitarScales@All-Guitar-Chords.com

www.jazzguitar.be

www.JustinsGuitar.com

www.myguitarsolo.com

www.superrockguitar.com

www.wholenote.com

http://www.wikihow.com/Be-a-Guitar-God

ADDITIONAL RESOURCES

WWW.ALLSTARSTRINGS.COM Here you will find guitars, amps, and links to other websites.

WWW.AMERICANMUSICAL.COM Here you will find all your musical needs at a good price.

WWW.DAVESGUITAR.COM Electric guitars, acoustic guitars, basses, amps—find them all here.

WWW.FENDER.COM One of the most popular guitars is Fender. Find all your fender needs here.

WWW.GIBSON.COM Gibson is another classic guitar. Find your Gibson guitars and accessories here.

WWW.GUITARBITZ.COM Amps, guitars, strings, effects pedals, guitar parts. This site rocks!

WWW.GUITARCENTER.COM A great website where you will find a wide selection of guitars.

WWW.GUITARGUITAR.COM Scotland's largest collection of guitars is right here. Stop by the store when you're in Edinburgh or you can just go online.

WWW.IBANEZ.COM Great guitarists like Steve Vai and Joe Satriani play Ibanez guitars.

WWW.MARTINGUITAR.COM If you're looking for an acoustic guitar, this site is a must.

WWW.MUSIC123.COM Finding your musical needs is as easy as 1,2,3 on this site.

WWW.MUSICIANSFRIEND.COM This site is truly a musician's friend.

WWW.SAMASH.COM Here you will find a wide selection of guitars, basses, drums, keyboards, live sound gear, recording gear, DJ & Lighting equipment, band/orchestra, books/DVD's and accessories.

WWW.SWEETWATER.COM This site offers a sweet supply of all your musical wants and needs.

WWW.VINTAGEGUITARANDBASS.COM If you're an old school type of guy or gal, check this site out.

WWW.ZZOUNDS.COM Guitars, accessories, basses, drums, recording equipment and so much more—this site is packed with the goods!

Glossary of Guitar and Musical Terms

3/4-SIZE GUITAR—A smaller than normal guitar with shorter strings and less space between frets.

ACTION—A term referring to the height of the strings above the frets and fretboard.

ALTERED AND OPEN TUNINGS—The result of changing the tuning of one or more strings from standard EADGBE.

ALTERNATE PICKING—Picking in alternate directions (down-up-down-up).

AMPLIFIER—Electronic equipment that increases strength of signals passing through it. In acoustic guitar amplification process an amplifier increase a line-level signal coming from a pre-amplifier.

ARPEGGIO—A broken chord, usually played evenly low to high and back again.

ARRANGEMENT—The setting of an original or standard tune for a given solo instrument or group of instruments

ARTIFICIAL HARMONIC—Hold down a note on the neck with left hand, and use the right hand to lightly touch a point on the string, then pluck the side of the string that is closer to the bridge. This technique is used to produce harmonic tones that are otherwise inaccessible. To guitar players, this technique is also known as a pinch harmonic.

BAR—A sub division of time in music

BAR LINE—A vertical line which shows the end of a bar of music.

BASS-STRUM STYLE—A right hand technique which involves picking a bass note then strumming the rest of the chord.

BARRE CHORD—From the French term *barré*. The technique of placing the left hand index finger over two to six strings in the fingering of a chord. The great advantage of using barre chords is that they are "moveable shapes" that can be applied at practically any fret.

BEAM—A horizontal line which shows two eighth or sixteenth notes belonging to the beat shown on the bottom of the time signature.

BEAT—A sub division of time usually felt as the pulse within a piece of music.

BENDING—The act of pushing or pulling a string sideways across the a fret to raise the pitch of a note by a half to full tone or more. Used extensively in rock and blues *playing* as well as in jazz.

BIGSBY—Term used for a simple non recessed vibrato developed by Paul Bigsby.

BPM—Beats per minute, or tempo. Defines the "click speed" of the metronome.

BRIDGE—The bridge is located on the body of the guitar and transfers sound from the strings to the body of the guitar. This can be held in place by screws or string tension.

CAPO—A mechanical barre that attaches to the neck of a guitar by means of a string, spring, elastic or nylon band, or a lever and thumbscrew arrangement. The capo can be used to raise the key of a song to suit a vocalist as well as to lower the action and shorten the string length.

CHORD—Three or more notes sounded simultaneously.

CHORD CHART— A diagram which shows a chord progression.

CHORD PROGRESSION—A sequence of chords played one after another.

CHORUS (of a tune)—Strictly speaking, the portion of a song lyric or melody that is repeated, often with other voices joining in. In jazz improvisation, however, "playing a chorus" would mean taking a turn improvising over the tune's chords progression.

CLOSED VOICING—The term "voicing" refers to the vertical arrangement of the notes of a given chord. "Closed voicing" places the member notes as close together as possible, no matter the inversion as opposed to "open voicing" which spreads the member notes of the chord at larger intervals.

CHROMATICS—12-note scale including all the semitones of the octave.

CHROMATIC SCALE- Because the chromatic scale has twelve notes and each fret on the guitar moves up one half-step, every note appears on all six strings somewhere before the twelfth fret. In other words, there is an 'E' on every string, an 'A' on every string, a 'Gb' on every string, etc.

CUTAWAY—A concave area generally in the upper right bout of a normal right-hand guitar that allows the player easier access to the high frets.

DOUBLE BAR LINE—Two vertical lines which show the end of a section or piece of music.

DOUBLE STOP—two notes played simultaneously.

DOWN STROKE—Right hand movement from top to bottom.

DROPPED-D TUNING—The practice of lowering the sixth string (E) by a whole tone, one octave lower than the fourth string.

FIFTH STRING—The fifth string of a standard 6-string guitar is the fifth one when you start counting from the bottom of you fingerboard. Why the fifth string matters? In standard tuning, it is tuned on the 440Hz frequency (A-440)

FINGER PICKS—Banjo-style picks that fingerstyle guitarists use when playing steel-string instruments.

FINGERBOARD—A strip of wood on the neck of a stringed musical instrument against which the strings are pressed in by fingers.

FINGERSTYLE—Playing with the fingernails or fingertips with or without fingerpicks as opposed to playing with a flatpick.

FIRST STRING—First string at the bottom of the fingerboard (and not the first string you see when you are playing)—You will share on your tuning from the 6th to the 1st string

FLAT—Lower in pitch.

FLATPICK—A triangular or teardrop-shaped piece of nylon or plastic used to pluck or strum guitar strings. Flatpicks are available in a large variety of shapes, sizes, and thickness.

FOOTSTOOL—A small adjustable stool used to raise the height of the guitar.

FOUR/FOUR TIME—A time signature of four quarter beats in one bar of music.

FRET—Metal bar placed on the fingerboard

FRETBOARD—Fretted fingerboard

FRET MARKER—Any marking on the fretboard to assist the guitarist to quickly locate a particular fret. Fret markers are typically found at frets 3, 5, 7, 9, 12, 15, and 17. Fret twelve is usually marked differently, to indicate the octave fret. Many guitars have small fret markers on the side of the neck, for easy reference as you look down while playing.

FRETTING—Placing a finger next to a fret.

HAMMER-ON—A note sounded literally by "hammering" down with a left hand finger, often performed in conjunction with a note first plucked by the right hand on the same string.

HARMONICS—Chime-like sounds achieved in two ways: 1) *natural harmonics*—by touching a string at any equidistant division of the string length (typically 5th, 7th, and 12th fret), directly above the fret with left hand, and striking hard with the right-hand fingers or pick near the bridge where there is more string resistance; or 2) *artificial harmonics*—touching a string with the index finger of the right hand twelve frets higher than any fretted note and plucking the string with either the thumb or third finger of the right hand.

HARMONIZE—To bring two or notes together in harmony.

HARMONY—Two or more notes sounding simultaneously.

HEXATONIC SCALE—A scale with six notes per octave (a pentatonic scale has five notes per octave).

INTERVAL—The distance between two notes.

INTONATION—The ability of your instrument to play and hold the correct note. Often adjusted by adjusting the bridge saddle.

IN TUNE—A note is in-tune when it matches the pitch of another note in the manner it is supposed to. When tuning a guitar, strings are "in tune" with each other when you can sound the same note on different strings and they sound the same. When playing a chord, a note is in tune if it sounds at the right interval from the other notes around it.

INVERSION—Structuring a chord with a note other than the root as the lowest note.

LEAD GUITAR—The part played by a guitar soloist in a rock band

LEGATO—Is obtained on the guitar by using strictly hammer-ons and pull-offs.

LUTHIER—A guitar maker and guitar repair expert. Always look for an experienced luthier. A good luthier will generally offer free repair estimates and explain the nature of the repair. Sometimes incorrectly spelled Luther

MAJOR CHORD—The combination of the first, third and fifth notes of a scale.

MELODY—A succession of musical notes played one after another (usually the most recognizable tune of a song).

MODULATE—To change keys within a piece of music

NECK—The part of a guitar which houses the fret board. The neck is sort of the middle of the guitar. It's where the strings are stretched over the fretboard.

NOTE—A note is defined by it's frequency: the speed of vibration of the sound producing device. For a guitar, the vibration is created by the strings.

NUT—Piece of plastic or metal between the headstock and fretboard. Guides the strings from the headstock and tuners over the fretboard.

OCTAVE—A simplified definition is: eight notes in sequence. Technically, this definition is only true if you think of notes by their name. For example, the notes C-D-E-F-G-A-B-C form an octave from C to C. More specifically, an octave is any two tones with frequency ratios of either 2-to-1 or 1-to-2.

OPEN—A string played with no left hand fingers fretting any note.

OPEN CHORDS—These chords usually contain open strings (not fretted with left hand). Often the first kind of chords the beginner will learn (D—C—Am etc). The opposite of barre- or power chords.

OPEN VOICING—A manner of chord construction in which the member notes are broadly separated.

OUT OF TUNE—Anything not "in tune" is, by definition "out of tune."

OPEN VOICING—A manner of chord construction in which the member notes are broadly separated. See *closed voicing* above.

PALM MUTE—The string(s) is being damped with right hand palm, close to the guitar's bridge

PEDAL TONES—Notes that constantly repeat in a pattern. This technique is favored by neoclassical guitarist such as Yngwie Malmsteen, Vinnie Moore etc.

PENTATONIC SCALE—A five-tone scale used often in rock.

PICKING—Plucking or producing a sound on the guitar in general, either with the fingers or a flatpick. Sometimes refers to playing a single-note melody line.

p i m a—letters derived from the Spanish names for the fingers of the right hand: *pulgar* (thumb), *indice* (index), *medio* (middle), and *anular* (ring). Used to indicate fingering.

PINCH HARMONIC—The thumb slightly catches the string after it is picked, creating a high pitched sound in any position. Usually requires heavily distorted amplifier settings. Pinch harmonics are also known as artificial harmonics.

PLECTRUM—Another name for a flatpick.

POSITIONS—A reference to placement of the left hand index finger at various frets.

POWER CHORD—A chord consisting of the first (root), fifth and eighth degree (octave) of the scale. Power chords are typically used in playing rock music.

PRE-BEND—The note is bend before it is struck with the pick. Make sure the note is bend to the right pitch.

PULL-OFF—The opposite of a hammer-on. Performed by plucking a note with a finger on a higher note and pulling parallel to the fret to sound a lower note on the same string.

REPEAT SIGN—Two dots placed before a double line indicating the repeat of a section of music

RHYTHM GUITAR—Rhythmic strumming of chord backup for a lead player, singer, or ensemble.

ROOT—The first note of a scale. A chord is named for it's root, even if the root is not actually played.

SETUP—The adjustment of the action of a guitar for optimal playing characteristics.

SHARP—Higher in pitch.

SIX STRING—Shorthand for a guitar that has six strings. Most acoustic and electric guitars have six strings, some have twelve.

LIDE—A plastic or glass tube placed over the third or fourth finger of the left hand and used to play "slide" or glissando effects in rock and blues and other forms of traditional music.

SLUR—To glide over (a series of notes) smoothly without a break, often used in combination with legato.

SLIDE—A plastic or glass tube placed over the third or fourth finger of the left hand and used to play "slide" or glissando effects in rock and blues and other forms of traditional music.

STACCATO—Is obtained on the guitar by using strictly alterntate picking.

STANDARD TUNING- A six-string guitar tuned to E-A-D-G-B-E, or a bass tuned to E-A-D-G. Most beginners learn in standard tuning.

STEM—The vertical line in music or rhythm notation which appears above or below a note or rhythm.

STRING WINDER—A swivel device with a handle with a fixture that fits over the tuning keys.

STRUMMING—Performed with a pick or the fingers. Generally consists of brushing across 2-6 strings in a rhythmic up and down fashion appropriate to the tune being played.

SUSTAIN—The duration of sound from one or more strings. The longer a note, or notes, can be heard, the longer the sustain.

SWEEPING—The pick is swept through the strings in a down- or upwoard motion. This technique is used mainly used with arpeggios.

SYNCOPATE—To modify the rhythm by stressing or accenting a weak beat (purposely playing off beat).

TABLATURE OR TAB—A system of writing music for fretted instruments whereby a number or letter appears on lines representing the strings, indicating the fret to be played.

TAPPING—The use of right hand fingers on the fretboard, I recomend the middle finger, so that you don't have to put down the pick.

TEMPO—The speed of a piece of music.

THREE/FOURTIME—A time signature of three quarter beats in one bar of music.

TIE—A curved line which shows two notes of the same pitch joined together and played as one with the time value of both.

TIME SIGNATURE—A sign at the beginning of a piece of music (looks like a fraction) which shows how many beats in each bar (top number) and how long each beat lasts (bottom number).

TONE—The combination of pitch, volume, sustain and sound character produced by a particular guitar or guitar equipment.

TRANSCRIPTION—To write a solo, note for note, off of a recording.

TRANSPOSE—To change the key of a piece of music by a specific interval.

TREMOLO—A technique performed with either a very rapid down-up movement of the pick or a pami plucking of the fingers.

TRIAD—A three-note chord.

TUNER—An electronic tuning device.

TUNING—Adjusting the tuning keys until a particular string vibrates at the correct frequency, and sounds the proper note(s).

UP STROKE—Right hand movement from bottom to top.

VERSE—The lyrics " melody portion of a song that tell the flowing story. A chorus is usually sung after each verse.

VIBRATO—To vibrate by slightly altering a pitch higher and lower.

VOICING—The arrangement of the member notes of a chord, or placement of the melody or bass line within a harmonic progression.

WAIST—Part of the body of a guitar which is smallest in dimension from top to bottom.

WHAMMY BAR—Used to stretch the strings on a tremolo or vibrato system.

WHOLE BEAT—A beat in music which lasts for a whole bar in music with a time signature of four/four.

INDEX